CAMBRIDGE LIBRARY COLLECTION

Books of enduring scholarly value

Spiritualism and Esoteric Knowledge

Magic, superstition, the occult sciences and esoteric knowledge appear
regularly in the history of ideas alongside more established academic
disciplines such as philosophy, natural history and theology. Particularly
fascinating are periods of rapid scientific advances such as the Renaissance
or the nineteenth century which also see a burgeoning of interest in the
paranormal among the educated elite. This series provides primary texts and
secondary sources for social historians and cultural anthropologists working
in these areas, and all who wish for a wider understanding of the diverse
intellectual and spiritual movements that formed a backdrop to the academic
and political achievements of their day. It ranges from works on Babylonian
and Jewish magic in the ancient world, through studies of sixteenth-century
topics such as Cornelius Agrippa and the rapid spread of Rosicrucianism, to
nineteenth-century publications by Sir Walter Scott and Sir Arthur Conan
Doyle. Subjects include astrology, mesmerism, spiritualism, theosophy,
clairvoyance, and ghost-seeing, as described both by their adherents and by
sceptics.

On the Phenomena of Dreams

The distinguished surgeon and medical writer Walter Cooper Dendy
(1794–1871) published *On the Phenomena of Dreams* in 1832. The work
carefully traces the history of western thought and philosophy on the topic of
dreams and visions, examining authors from Aristotle to Hume and Pyrrho
to Berkeley, and maps the development of poetical and literary traditions
on the subject. Dendy's work then moves to an attempt to find a medical
explanation and material source for dreams, psychic visions and illusions.
Dendy presents his concept of a ghost as an intense idea, and attempts
to classify and categorise different types of psychic experiences. Dendy's
work was a pioneering attempt to find scientific solutions to supernatural
phenomena. Very popular at the time, it now offers an invaluable insight
into the Victorian fascination with the occult and the desire to approach the
supernatural with reason and the rigours of scientific investigation.

T0382125

Cambridge University Press has long been a pioneer in the reissuing of out-of-print titles from its own backlist, producing digital reprints of books that are still sought after by scholars and students but could not be reprinted economically using traditional technology. The Cambridge Library Collection extends this activity to a wider range of books which are still of importance to researchers and professionals, either for the source material they contain, or as landmarks in the history of their academic discipline.

Drawing from the world-renowned collections in the Cambridge University Library, and guided by the advice of experts in each subject area, Cambridge University Press is using state-of-the-art scanning machines in its own Printing House to capture the content of each book selected for inclusion. The files are processed to give a consistently clear, crisp image, and the books finished to the high quality standard for which the Press is recognised around the world. The latest print-on-demand technology ensures that the books will remain available indefinitely, and that orders for single or multiple copies can quickly be supplied.

The Cambridge Library Collection will bring back to life books of enduring scholarly value (including out-of-copyright works originally issued by other publishers) across a wide range of disciplines in the humanities and social sciences and in science and technology.

On the
Phenomena of Dreams

And Other Transient Illusions

WALTER COOPER DENDY

CAMBRIDGE UNIVERSITY PRESS

Cambridge, New York, Melbourne, Madrid, Cape Town,
Singapore, São Paolo, Delhi, Tokyo, Mexico City

Published in the United States of America by Cambridge University Press, New York

www.cambridge.org
Information on this title: www.cambridge.org/9781108073080

© in this compilation Cambridge University Press 2011

This edition first published 1832
This digitally printed version 2011

ISBN 978-1-108-07308-0 Paperback

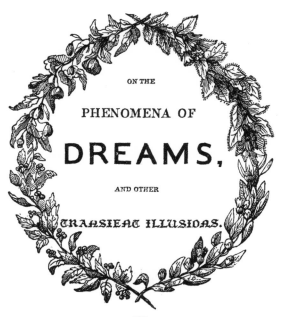

ON THE

PHENOMENA OF

DREAMS,

AND OTHER

TRANSIENT ILLUSIONS.

BY

WALTER C. DENDY,

MEMBER OF THE ROYAL COLLEGE OF SURGEONS IN LONDON;
FELLOW AND HONORARY SECRETARY OF THE MEDICAL
SOCIETY OF LONDON ; SURGEON TO THE ROYAL
INFIRMARY FOR THE DISEASES OF
CHILDREN, &c. &c.

LONDON:

WHITTAKER, TREACHER & Co.

AVE-MARIA-LANE.

1832.

PREFACE.

—

IF a prefatory apology were ever requisite, it must be for the presumption of offering a dissertation on a subject of deep metaphysical interest, on which the philosophical minds of Stewart and of Abercrombie have been so seriously engaged.

The following Essay was chiefly written before the excellent " Inquiries concerning the Intellectual Powers," were published. Their appearance, perhaps, should have immediately checked the scribbling of a more humble pathologist. The mind, however, which has been reflecting on an

interesting subject, but too readily yields
to a desire of formally recording its reflections, and of inflicting on others the result
of its study.

Some of the illustrations which I had
selected have been embodied in the " Inquiries," and in Sir Walter Scott's " Letters on Demonology ;" I have, therefore,
thought it essential to erase that portion
of them.

With a consciousness of the disparity
between the sublimity of my subject and
the extent of my own researches, I cannot
offer this Essay without fear that its
lighter parts may be deemed puerile, and
that its argument may too often incur the
censure of plagiarism.

Upper Stamford-street.

DREAMS.

———

———" We are such stuff
As dreams are made of, and our little life
Is rounded with a sleep."

TEMPEST.

OVER the intimate nature of mind crea-
tive wisdom has thrown a veil which even
the profound philosopher can never hope
to draw aside. Although the beautiful
mechanism of its organ may be apparent,
its phenomena are not, like most of the
organic functions of the body, demon-
strable. In the abstract study, in which
psycologists have been engaged, of this
sublime subject, they have failed in esta-
blishing satisfactory principles, because

B

the mind of the individual has been the
chief or only basis of the investigation.
Hence arise the contrasted hypotheses of
these philosophers—the *cogitation* of Des
Cartes—the *consciousness* of Locke—the
spiritualism of Berkeley—the *idealism* of
Hume. The *seat* of mind, however, is a
matter of almost universal belief, although
we know not the mode of connection, nor
the manner of their mutual influence. It
is into the brain that the nerves of all the
senses enter, or from which they emanate. As these senses then constitute the
sources from which the mind gains its
knowledge of the world, we regard the brain
as its seat. To the manifestations or functions of this high characteristic of human
nature, it will be necessary for me briefly to
allude, in attempting to explain those transient illusions of the mind, which arise
from a derangement of its operations. It
may be objected that the anatomy and
physiology of the mental organ should

be fully elucidated before we attempt to
reason on its pathology: as we consider
the brain, however, but as a medium for
the manifestations of mental phenomena, it
may not be inconsistent to refer to those
manifestations in connection with certain
conditions of the cerebral mass, without a
perfect investigation of its nature or its
modes of action, reserving the more minute
pathology until repeated dissections may
enable us to demonstrate the intimate causes
of its derangements, or at least to render
more perfect the physiology of brain. We
must be all painfully sensible of this truth
—that the most extensive lesions of brain
are often discovered, which previous symptoms had never indicated; and its converse—that the most severe and fatal disorders of mind have occurred—the brain
exhibiting on dissection little or no disorganization: indeed Dr. Baillie asserted this
result of his experience, that the disorganization of brain is commonly found in an

inverse ratio to the severity of symptoms.
In reference to the former instances, the
explanation may consist in the great ba-
lancing power of the *circulation* of the
brain, without which, the incompressibility
of its proper substance would subject it to
constant injury.   When chronic tumours
or cysts are formed gradually in the
brain, the quantity of blood will usually
be diminished in proportion.   In hydro-
cephalus also, the same circumstance may
occur.   The fact has been proved in com-
parative pathology.   The skull of a sheep
sent by Dr. Cholmeley was trephined by
Mr. Gosset.   On the escape of some
limpid fluid the brain appeared collapsed
on the base of the skull.   In a very short
time, however, it expanded and *filled* the
cranial cavity; not of course by rapid
growth, but by a rush of that volume of
blood which had been displaced.

Independent of the sense of self-feeling,
termed *caenlesthesis*, and by the Germans,

selbst-gefühl, the mind is thought to
possess five faculties—perception—association — memory — imagination — and
judgment.   The seat of all these faculties
—their concentration or focus, is the brain.
That to different parts of this organ are
allotted different functions can scarcely be
doubted ; the experiments of physiologists
are proofs of it ; indeed, when we look on
the varied structure of the interior of the
brain—on its intricate divisions—its eccentric, yet uniform cavities—its delicate
and almost invisible membranes—we cannot form any other conclusion, however
we may disregard the fanciful cranial topo-
graphy of Gall.   Brain, however, can no
more be considered as mind itself than
retina, sight ; or than the sealing-wax can
be identical with the electricity residing
in it.   It is the habitat of mind, and its
workings cannot be indicated without it ;
but it cannot properly be termed its origin,
as that word implies the office of a gland

—that the function of the brain was indeed
the secretion of thought.

It was the error of Priestley to suppose
that function and structure were identical,
because they are influenced by the same
disease, and seem to live and die, flourish
and decay, together. We must be conscious of the great difficulty of conceiving
the nature of spirit, but if we are required
to prove its existence, we may answer, by
analogy, that we cannot always palpably
prove the existence of matter, although
we know it to exist. The electric fluid
may remain for an indefinite period invisible, nay, may never meet the sight; it
may even traverse a space without any
evidence, but that of its wonderful influence, and at length be collected in a jar.
—So, if I may venture the simile, the principle of life, whatever it be, may seem to
have an independent existence even during
life, to leave the body and yet not perish.
The opinions of Priestley can only escape

the stigma of being supposed to favour
the doctrine of annihilation, by believing
that he adopted the system of the ancients
who recognised in man three great principles, Σωμα, ψυχη, and νους,—*i. e.* body,
soul, and mind; and that his arguments to
establish the identity of brain and mind
referred only to the νους, without pre-
suming to touch the sublime nature of the
ψυχη.

The more moderate materialist, who has
been perversely termed Pyrrhonian, will
not allow that the mind can have, during
the life of the body, even a momentary
existence independent of matter; and of
course, that when this matter is in a state
of perfect repose, mind is at the same time
perfectly passive. It was the opinion of
Paley, expressed in his discourse on a
future state, founded on New Testament
evidence, that we should have a substantial resurrection. Dr. Johnson expressed
this opinion in these words:—" We see
that it is not to be the same body, for the

Scripture uses the illustration of grain sown; and we know that the grain which grows is not the same with what is sown. You cannot suppose that we shall rise with a diseased body ; it is enough if there be such a sameness as to distinguish identity of person [1]." And Blumenbach believed that when the soul revived after death, the brain would equally revive. This eternal union bears closely on the subject, but, without digressing further, I would generally adopt the precept of Lord Bacon, that the physical enquirer should waive theology in his researches, because I am unwilling to mingle the sacred truths of spiritual futurity with arguments on the imperfection of material existence. It is evident, that although not identical, the brain and mind exist in the most intimate union. The ultra spiritualist has attempted, however, to undervalue this relative influence—to disprove the decay of mind

---

[1] Boswell's Life of Johnson, vol. iv. 88.

according to the age of the body, by ad-
ducing the energy of intellect, and the
brilliancy of conception which Cicero,
Plato, and Newton possessed in advanced
life. These, however, are exceptions to a
general rule, for as the lives of different
persons are of different duration, and as
the integrity and energy of bodily constitutions vary, so may the mental powers
be, even *cæteris paribus,* of very different
degrees of vigour.

In our investigation of the illusion of
mind, the relative exercise of its faculties
is a subject of the highest interest; it
forms the groundwork of my Essay. The
essence of the condition of mind consists
in the possession of any one or more of
the faculties excepting that of *judgment.*
Whatever, then, may exert that influence
over the mind as to destroy the integrity
or suspend the action of this faculty, is
the exciting cause of illusion.

As there can scarcely be found one body

in a state of perfect health, so are there few minds in which these causes are not occasionally influential : the phenomena being more or less transient as the condition of the brain may be less or more disturbed.

I have drawn a decided distinction between insanity and the subject of this essay — *transient* illusion. — The phenomena may occasionally bear a strong resemblance, nay, by casual observers, may appear identical, but it is in one most essential point that they differ, viz. that the transient derangement is not manifested except during a condition of sleep or slumber, or a state closely analogous to it.

The immediate cause of sleep appears to consist in certain conditions of the blood in the vessels of the brain, depending on the reflux of a great portion of the vital fluid towards the heart as in deliquium, or its congestion in the sinusses or veins. This condition may result from depressed

nervous energy, exhaustion, fatigue, cold,
or the influence of powerful narcotics;
and when either of these causes is in
excess, death itself is the result.   Deep
sleep indeed is truly

" Mortis imago et simulacrum."

Or, as Milton has most elegantly expressed
it—

——————————" There gentle sleep
First found me, and with soft oppression seiz'd
My drowned sense, untroubled, tho' I thought
I then was passing to my former state,
Insensible, and forthwith to dissolve."

Par. Lost, viii. 283.

In these allusions we must only regard
the mind as it is concerned with a sublunary state, and not approximate even the
dangerous sentiments which Boswell has
ascribed to Miss Seward.—" There is one
mode of the fear of death which is certainly absurd, and that is the dread of

annihilation, which is only a pleasing
sleep, without a dream [1]."

Sleep, then, is only a term to express
that condition which is marked by a cessation of certain mental manifestations, co-
incident with the degree of oppression.
Thus is it contrasted with a state of waking, an activity of mind, in which ideas
are constantly chasing each other like
the waves of Ocean; the mode of dis-
placing one idea being by the excitement
of another in its place.

Professor Stewart thought that there
was a total suspension of volition during
sleep; the position must be granted with
regard to sound sleep, though not to
slumber, or that state produced by lulling
sounds, the gentle motions of a swing, a
carriage, or a cradle; the exhibition of a
mild anodyne, or that peculiar state of
vertigo produced by the influence of Mes-

---

[1] Boswell's Life of Johnson, vol. iii. 284.

merism [1]. But is volition always suspended, even in sound sleep? The fact

[1] Mesmerism, or animal magnetism, appears to be
essentially a variety of chorea, the symptoms excited
being almost as varied. Vertigo, syncope, and religious ecstacy are certainly produced by its vaunted influence, but its full development, its presumed *mystery*,
requires the predisposition of faith.

That peculiar feeling caused by the "busy hum of
men," by which the mind is lulled, as it were, into abstraction, is of a similar nature. Hence some contem-
plative philosopher has observed, that man is never so
much alone, as in the midst of a populous city.

Dr. Marcus Herz, in his "Essay on Vertigo," ob-
serves that a certain period must elapse ere an external object makes a complete impression on the mind.
If many objects are hurried past the eyes, or sounds
succeed each other in a rapid manner, our perception
is only imperfectly influenced by them, and the mind
would be thus left to employ itself without interruption,
as if its senses were shut. This rapid succession of
representations is usually, however, so powerful as to
overcome attention; but if reflection or attention on
one object be exercised to a certain degree, the verti-
ginous feeling may be resisted, and the whole mystery
of Mesmerism be dissolved. It matters not on what

that a predetermination to awake at a
certain hour, produces so strong an impression on the mind as to cause the
breaking of sleep almost at the given
moment, may not at first be very easily
explained without the admission of volition.   We have, however, some very curious instances of the regular periodical
recurrence of ideas, in a *waking* state, in
which the phenomena cannot be altogether explained on the principle of volition,
the exactness of the measurement of time
being referrible to the nature of mental
impression mechanically established by
constant habit.   Thus we are told of an
Idiot, who was constantly amusing himself by counting the hours as they were
struck on the clock : the works of the

sense these quick successions are produced : the retina, the schneiderian membrane, or the expansion of
the portio mollis of the auditory nerve.   If the mind
cannot follow those impressions, so as properly to
associate them, it becomes confused, and the magnetic
ecstacy ensues.

clock having become damaged, the idiot,
notwithstanding, continued to measure
the day by counting and beating the
hour at the exact period [1].

In a state of sleep, of that sound sleep
which overcomes children and persons of
little reflection, the mind is probably perfectly quiescent, and its manifestations
cease. That these manifestations are intimately dependent on organization few will
doubt. This dependence cannot be more
decidedly proved, than by a necessity for
the occasional repose of the mental organ.

"Non semper arcum tendit Apollo."

In some morbid constitutions these indi-
cations are most frequent, most decided,
and distressing : all the efforts and philosophical determination to overcome the
depression only adding to its intensity.
This conflict cannot be more pertinently
exemplified than by some passages in the

[1] Vide History of Staffordshire, by Dr. Plot.

life of Collins, by one who knew him
well.

" He languished some years under that
depression of mind which unchains the
faculties without destroying them, and
leaves reason the knowledge of right without the power of pursuing it. These
clouds, which he perceived gathering on
his intellects, he endeavoured to disperse
by travel, and passed into France; but
found himself constrained to yield to his
malady, and returned. His disorder was
no alienation of mind, but general laxity
and feebleness, a deficiency rather of his
vital than intellectual powers. What he
spoke wanted neither judgment nor spirit;
but a few minutes exhausted him, so that
he was forced to rest upon the couch, till
a short cessation restored his powers, and
he was again able to talk with his former
vigour [1]."

[1] Johnson's Lives of the Poets.

The mind, then, cannot exert itself beyond a certain period without a sensation of fatigue, as palpable as the exhaustion from excessive muscular exertion. Muscular fibre, however, will regain its expenditure by simple rest, but the excitement of thought beyond certain limits is both painful and destructive, evincing its effects by various grades of mental disorder, from simple head-ache to confirmed mania. Its immediate remedy is sleep,

———————————" The innocent sleep,
Sleep that knits up the ravelled sleeve of care,
The death of each day's life, sore labour's bath,
Balm of hurt minds."—MACBETH.

The ordinary employment of intellect is not of course to so great a degree detrimental, but the mind, which had been exerting itself during waking hours, in planning, calculating, comparing, in one word, reflecting, seeks relief from the consequent exhaustion in sleep.

c

Beyond our thankfulness for this balmy slumber we could almost echo the rhapsody of Sancho Panza,

" Blessed is he who first invented sleep."

when we reflect that the most energetic mind must speedily sink without it, that we must, as is more intensely exemplified in delirium tremens, either sleep or die.

During the transition to and from this essential repose, the intellect itself will be in an impaired state—its evidences imperfect. The faculty of comparing ideas, the judgment, loses its control. Notwithstanding this, although the active power of drawing conclusions may be suspended, there is sometimes a sort of involuntary reasoning, from a series of former impressions on the same subject; a property of mind which must not be considered as analogous to reflection. Involuntary or unreflecting *memory* is, in regard to volition, passive—it may be instinctive—*re-*

collection, on the contrary, is an effort depending on volition. To this effect it has been shrewdly remarked, " Beasts and babies remember, man alone *recollects.*"

It is evident, then, that slumber possesses the power of destroying the relative consistency of those mental faculties which are not absolutely suspended. The mind, when excited during this state, may possess the power of exercising the faculties of perception, association, memory, or imagination, individually or collectively, but the influence of *judgment* over the ideas thus excited being lost, imperfect conclusions are formed : in this want of integrity consists the most common species of transient illusion, Dreaming.

The dream, I believe, never occurs in sound or perfect sleep, for then all the senses are quiescent or uninfluenced, at least by slight stimuli : to rouse the person loud sounds and powerful light are requisite. It is produced in that state which we denominate *slumber*, the period of transition from waking to sleep, or from sleep to waking, the moments of departing or returning consciousness.

But it will be thought, perhaps, that I am reversing the order of these phenomena,—that, in fact, the excitement of vague ideas in the mind is itself the *cause* of waking. I believe that this is not the case, except the sensibility of the body be influenced by touch or sound, or by congestions of blood in the brain, causing that state of disturbance which reduces sound sleep to slumber, as in the instance of night-mare, which is to the mind what sensation is to the body, restoring the mind to that state of half consciousness which is essential to the phenomena of dreaming [1].

[1] Sir Walter Scott alludes to this notion in the Anti-

The state of sound sleep that

" Certissima mortis imago,"

is incompatible even with consciousness,
(by which I do not mean sensibility to
touch, or to stimuli,) and *à fortiori*, with
the slightest exercise of the faculty of
judgment. This notion has been poeti-
cally expressed in Jachimo's invocation
in the chamber of Imogen,

" Oh sleep, thou ape of Death, lie dull upon her,
    And be her sense but as a monument
    Thus in a chapel lying."

It has been asserted, however, especially by two profound metaphysicians,
Beattie and Reid, that they persuaded
themselves in their dreams that they *were*
dreaming, and would then attempt to
throw themselves off a precipice ; this

quary :—" Eh, Sirs, sic weary dreams as folk hae between sleeping and waking, before they win to the lang
sleep and the sound."

awoke them, and proved the impression a
fiction.

I presume that the condition in which
these philosophers then were placed, was
under the influence of Incubus. The
phenomena, nay, the expressions which
are used to relate them, are precisely illustrative of the condition of night-mare.
When, therefore, Dr. Beattie asserts that
he *knew* he was dreaming, his mind, I
believe, was labouring under that oppressive congestion compatible with consciousness.

If we *know* that we are dreaming, the
faculty of judgment cannot be inert, which
I believe it is in the Dream ; and in support of my opinion I would adduce the
following anecdote of Dr. Johnson : " He
related that he had once, in a dream, a
contest of wit with some other person, and
that he was very much mortified by ima-
gining that his opponent had the better of
him. ' Now,' said he, ' one may mark

here the effect of sleep in weakening the
power of reflection, for had not my judgment failed me, I should have seen that
the wit of this supposed antagonist, by
whose superiority I felt myself depressed,
was as much furnished by me as that
which I thought I had been uttering in my
own character.' "

It is not uncommon for the dreamer to
reverse the doctrine of Pyrrho, who doubted
his own existence, and to imagine himself
possessed of ubiquity—to be both old and
young at the same moment—to possess
the hundred eyes of Argus, or the hundred
hands of Briareus. In short, he is influenced in thought and action by a complete principle of paradox—to form a fresh
creation, an independent world of his own.
It was a saying I believe of Heraclitus,
that all men, whilst they are awake, are in
one common world, but that each of them,
when he is asleep, is in a world of his
own.

Addison has added, that " there seems
something in this consideration that inti-
mates to us a natural grandeur and perfection in the soul, which is rather to be
admired than explained." I am not so
certain that these illusions tend to advance
our notion of the dignity of mind. Nothing can be more convincing to prove a
suspension of judgment. Still there is so
much impression made by these eccentric
dreams that intense pleasure or pain may
be felt by their recollection, during waking moments. Ambition may for a time
appear to have been fully gratified, im-
mense riches to have been gathered. On
the principle, therefore, that sublunary
happiness consists in our being agreeably
deceived, a perpetual dream would doubtless be, according to its subject, a state of
happiness or misery. On the contrary,
the dream may leave the most painful impression of disappointment on the memory:

thus Milton writes in his sonnet on a
dream of his dead wife—

" But oh ! as to embrace me she inclin'd,
I waked—she fled, and day brought back my night."

In other cases a void or solitude is felt
that may be most distressing.

———————————" She seems alone
To wander in her sleep thro' ways unknown,
Guideless and dark."
DRYDEN's Æneid, iv.

When the vivid sensation, from the
memory of a pleasant dream, has ceased,
there may still be pleasure to the dreamer
on his narration of the vision. Like the
mere verbal description of a landscape, it
will not excite, of course, any similar
delight in the mind of the hearer. Epic-
tetus has left us a caution regarding this
infliction.

"Never tell thy dream, for though thou
thyself mayest take a pleasure in telling

thy dream, another will take no pleasure in hearing it."

But we have more decided proofs of the *imperfection* of mental manifestation during our slumbers. In the words of Beattie—

" Sleep has a wonderful power over all our faculties. Sometimes we seem to have lost our moral faculty, as when we dream of doing that without scruple or remorse which, when awake, we could not bear to think of. Sometimes memory is extinguished, as when we dream of conversing with our departed friends, without remembering any thing of their death, though it was perhaps one of the most striking incidents we had ever experienced, and is seldom or never out of our thoughts when we are awake [1]."

In reasoning on the causes or nature of dreams, we must discard the sophisms of the pseudo psychologists, who consider the

---

[1] Essay on Truth.

dream as the uninfluenced and independent flight of soul; and, as a convincing proof of an immaterial mind during life, and of the existence of the soul itself; a sublime and internally evident truth, which requires not the support of such arguments.

According to these notions a dream may be the flight of the soul on a visit to other regions and its observations of their systems from actual survey. Of the fruits of this aerial voyage the dreamer is made conscious when the soul returns to the brain, its earthly pabulum or home; or to the pineal gland itself, which Des Cartes believed to be its sanctum sanctorum [1]. This hypothesis agrees with the doctrine of Petronius,

————" cum prostrata sopore
Urget membra quies et *mens sine pondere ludit* [2]."

---

[1] This belief rested on erroneous pathology. Des Cartes thought the gland was seldom found diseased, whereas a gritty matter is very frequently discovered in its substance.

[2] " While sleep oppresses the tir'd limbs, the mind
Plays without weight and wantons unconfined."

a sentiment which Addison has so readily adopted; prating about " the amuse-
ments of the soul when she is disencum-
bered of her machine," and so forth. An
illustration this of Plato's notion regarding
the existence of eternal forms independent
of matter, an emanation of the divine
mind imparted to that of human beings—
the doctrine of *innate idea,* by which the
mind views at large

"The uncreated images of things !"

There cannot be *any* thought or action
without this sublime emanation, " 'Tis the
divinity which stirs within us."

But although it must be confessed that
all dreams are not recollected or recorded,
it is clear that we have seldom very distinct self-satisfactory notions of having
actually, through the medium of the immaterial spirit, paid these visits—no remem-
brances of cities or temples which we are
conscious of having surveyed—no wonders
or eccentricities which eclipse the exploits

of Gulliver, Peter Wilkins, and Baron
Munchausen. Sir Thomas Brown, the
ingenious author of the " Religio Medici,"
surpasses these notions, when he writes :
—" We are somewhat more than ourselves
in our sleeps, and the slumber of the body
seems to be but the waking of the soul. It
is the ligation of sense, but the liberty of
reason, and our waking conceptions do not
match the fancies of our sleeps [1]."

This identifying of reason and fancy is
itself a proof of error. The energy of the
first is exercised in the consideration of
certain data or facts laid before it; the
other is employed in less than hypothetical
amusement—mere speculation.

" All power of fancy over reason is a
degree of insanity. By degrees the reign

---

[1] These metaphysical pathologists yet talk fluently
of *diseases* of the *immaterial* mind, forgetful it would
seem of the danger of their argument. That which is
diseased may die—a consummation which would blight
the holiest hope of man, the prospect of immortality.

of fancy is confirmed, she grows first im-
perious, and in time despotic. Then fictions begin to operate as realities, false
opinions fasten upon the mind, and life
passes in dreams of rapture or of anguish[1]."

It were much better that the hypothesis
of Berkeley were established, that nature
was but a compound of spirits, ideas unfet-
tered by matter,—or the visionary scheme
of Hume, "that there is nought but impression and idea in nature," or even the absolute scepticism of Pyrrho, than that this
rhapsody of Brown should be favoured—
that the consciousness of waking moments
should thus deteriorate reason, and render
the mind incompatible with sublunary
duties.

This absurd hypothesis of dreaming has
formed the basis of certain religious impostures; among others the fanatical vi-

---

[1] Rasselas. Chap. xix.

sions of Emanuel Swedenborg, and Santa
Teresa, who founded their especial sects,
by their impious declarations of having
visited Heaven.

The arguments which I have alluded
to are favouring the doctrine of *metempsy-
chosis* or transmigration of souls, which
it were a libel on reason to receive in any
other light than allegory; for instance, to
adduce the incomparable biography of
Queen Mab as an illustration of the metaphysical creed. If a disciple of Pytha-
goras were now to appear among us, we
should consider him only eligible to become an inmate of St. Luke's, however
classically he might vociferate—

———————————— " Errat et illinc
Huc venit, huic illuc, et quoslibet occupat artus,
Spiritus : eque feris humana in corpora transit,
Inque feras noster."

The stories of Fadlallah and the Dervis,
and the transmigrations of Indus, are

amusing fictions, in illustration of Mr.
Locke's notions on this most subtle point;
—viz. that it is consciousness and not corporeal identity, which constitutes personal
identity, or individuality.

Contrasted with the notions of spiritual
flight, we have certain philosophers who
assume *ideas*, or *thoughts* themselves to
be material. Among these is Lucretius,
the Epicurean, who, having asserted his
credence in apparitions, accounts for them
thus—that the surfaces of bodies are constantly thrown off by a sort of centrifugal
force; that an exact image is often presented to us by this surface coming off, as
it were, entire, like the cast skin of the
rattle-snake, or the shell of the chrysalis,
and thus these ideas of our absent or dead
friends *strike* on the mind. It was the
opinion of Lavater that it might be the
transportive imagination of the dead which
makes them appear in dreams to the living. And Dr. Darwin, in his Zoonomia,

tells us that ideas are " motions of
fibres."

" There is nothing," says Charlevoix,
" in which these barbarians, (the northern
Indians,) carry their superstition farther
than in what regards dreams; but they
vary greatly in their manner of explaining
themselves on this point. Sometimes it is
the reasonable soul which ranges abroad,
while the sensitive continues to animate
the body. Sometimes it is the familiar
genius who gives salutary counsel with
respect to what is going to happen. Sometimes it is a visit made by the soul of the
object of which he dreams [1]."

These are mere fallacies. In the words
of Des Cartes, " In dreams we often mistake ideas for external things really existing."

The dream may be excited either previous or subsequent to sleep, and there

---

[1] Charlevoix—Journal of a Voyage to North America.

D

are some persons who never fail to dream
during those slumbers. It does not appear that there is any certain relative
difference between the subjects of dreams
before and after sleep ; yet as far as I have
learned, there is more consistency—more
reference to real occurrence in the first, and
more confusion or wandering of the imagination in the second or morning dream.
Sound sleep, it is true, shall often be
broken by pain or uneasiness occurring in
a particular part of the body : the dream
at the period of slumber, or the transition
to waking, shall then bear an intimate
reference to the seat and nature of the
physical pain. If, for instance, cramp has
attacked any of the limbs, or the head has
been long confined back, the dream may
be enlivened by some analogous tortures
in the dungeons of the inquisition [1]. Pro-

---

[1] Hippocrates even applies this principle to the
detection of diseases, of which certainly the *patient*
himself can seldom form any notion from *sensation.*

fessor Stewart writes thus :—"1 have been told by a friend that, having occasion, in consequence of indisposition, to apply a bottle of hot water to his feet when he went to bed, he dreamed that he was making a journey to the top of Mount Ætna, and that he found the heat of the ground almost insupportable. Another person, having a blister applied to the head, dreamed that he was scalped by a party of Indians."

In the morbid condition of hypochondriasis, similar diseased perceptions will frequently occur. Hypochondriacs sometimes express themselves convinced of having frogs or serpents, or a concourse of persons, or even demons and evil spirits, pent up within. It will be proved that these errors of imagination usually arise from real sensation, as flatulence, dyspep-

---

He alludes to the dreaming about lakes, seas, and rivers, as an indication of hydrothorax, and others have considered such dreams as symptomatic of effusion on the brain.

sia, spasm, &c.   Cases of this description
are recorded in Bertholini, Hist. Anat. Var.

If the attention of the *waking* mind be
directed to a diseased and painful part, the
sensibility of such part is usually increased
by this attention.   (Such persons are ad-
vised in common parlance not to think
about it—not to brood over their troubles.)
So the brain is rendered peculiarly sensitive in the state of dreaming, by the intense
thought which the mind had exerted previous to the slumber; and the dream will
frequently coincide with the disposition
or sentiments indulged in previous to
sleep.   Persons affected with *nostalgia* are
frequently presented with visions of *home*
during their slumbers, and their sensibility
will be relieved by tears, as that of the
Swiss at the chime of the Rans des Vaches.

I believe that the period of time occupied
in a dream is usually exceedingly limited:
that like the wonderful velocity of atoms
of light, the crude and heterogeneous

ideas of a dream succeed each other with incalculable rapidity. The time occupied in the dream is often very far short of the seeming duration of a scene. We appear to have travelled over a series of miles, or to have existed for a series of years, during a minute portion of the night; how diminutive a period, it is perhaps impossible to determine.

Mallebranche has asserted, "that it is possible some creatures may think half an hour as long as we do a thousand years; or look upon that space of duration which we call a minute, as an hour, a week, a month, or a whole age." If this be correct, and Mr. Locke be borne out in his observation " that we get the idea of time or duration by reflecting on that train of ideas which succeed one another in our minds," it will then be easy to conceive that when this course of reflection is impeded, the measurement of time must be imperfect and erroneous.

I should perhaps apologize for the introduction of any thing like an imputed miracle, or imposture into this Essay; but a passage in the Alcoran, which is repeated in the Spectator, is so illustrative of my opinion, that I cannot forbear quoting it as a simple allegory.

It is there said, " that the angel Gabriel took Mahomet out of his bed one morning to give him a sight of all things in the seven heavens, in Paradise and in Hell, which the prophet took a distinct view of; and after having held ninety thousand conferences with God, was brought back again to his bed. All this, says the Alcoran, was transacted in so small a space of time, that Mahomet at his return found his bed still warm [1]."

Although our comprehension of the apparent anachronism of such dreams concludes it to be arising from imperfect

[1] Spectator, v. 2.

function, yet it is to be remembered that
we are reasoning as finite beings ; but in
regard to the prospect of futurity, of a
more perfect state, who of us can decide
that this seeming illusion is not one evidence of the divine nature of mind,—a
remote resemblance, if I may presume so
to write, of one attribute of the Creator, to
whom a thousand years are as one day?

After these remarks, then, I would presume to offer some rationale of my subject,
and would venture to assume that the
Dream consists in a *want of balance between the representative faculty and the
judgment,* being produced directly or in-
directly by the excitement of a chain of
ideas from impressions of memory, rational
or probable, in parts, but rendered in different degrees extravagant and illusive by
imperfect association.

If we grant that certain faculties or
functions of the mind are the result of
nervous influence, we can as readily allow
that an imperfection of these manifesta-

tions shall be the result of derangement of equilibrium of this influence, as the material function of muscle shall be disturbed by primary or secondary disease about the brain, of which we have daily examples among the spasmodic and nervous diseases of the body.

Although the ideas arising in slumber may truly be considered as a species of delirium, forming figures and situations of the most heterogeneous description, yet if the most absurd dream be analysed, its constituent parts will generally be proved to consist of ideas in themselves not irrational, or of sensations or incidents which have been individually felt or witnessed. Even the remembered faces and forms of our absent friends, faithful though a part of the likeness may be, are associated in circumstances of the grossest absurdity :

> " —— —— velut ægri somnia vanæ
> Fingentur species[1]."

[1] " As in a sick man's dream, incongruous shapes are presented."

The individual images in this chain may
bear an intimate relationship with each
other, although the first and last may appear perfectly incongruous; as the Chinese
puzzle will be a chaos, if its pieces be
wrongly placed.

Impressions of memory may not perhaps
appear consistent with imagination; but
on the principle I have advanced it will
be found, that although the ideas excited
by memory may be consistent, these ideas
may by fanciful association become imagination, appearing on superficial view to
illustrate the doctrine of innate idea. But
is this doctrine proved? We may seem to
imagine that which we do not remember
as a whole; but as a curve is made up of
right lines—as a mass is composed of an
infinity of atoms, so may it follow that
what is termed innate idea, if minutely
divided, may be proved to arise from
memory,—made up of things, however

minute, which we have seen or heard of.
Analysis may thus unravel many a "strange
mysterious dream."

Dr. Beattie has observed, " Men born
blind, or who have lost all remembrance
of light and colours, are as capable of
invention, and dream as frequently as those
who see [1]." But these surely are imperfect
data.   If a person loses remembrance of
individual colour, he does not lose the
power of comparing or of judging *variety*
of colour.   And again, although he may
be congenitally blind, yet if there be any
other sense but sight through which the
mind can perceive or receive external impression, the objection must fail.

Sir Walter Scott, in his Letters on
Demonology and Witchcraft, informs us,
that " those experienced in the education
of the deaf and dumb, find that their

---

[1] Essay on Truth.

pupils, even when cut off from all instruction by ordinary means, have been able to
form, out of their own unassisted conjec-
tures, some ideas of the existence of a
deity, and of the distinction between the
soul and body." But, again, may we
not affirm, that before the deaf and dumb
pupil can adopt a language by which to
make his preceptor sensible of his thoughts
or sentiments, he must have had certain
facts or knowledge imparted to *him* by
signs or other modes of instruction. The
modes of mutual understanding must first
emanate from the tutor, and with these,
ideas may be excited which at first sight
may seem to be innate or *unassisted*. If it
were possible to find a creature so wretched
as to be endued with no external sense
from his birth, such a being would neither
dream nor think—he would lead the life
almost of a Zoophyte. On the opening or
restoration of his senses, all his associations would be erroneous. He might, like

children, consider all bodies, however distant, within his grasp, and, like the idiot, draw all his figures topsy turvy, as they are really painted on the retina. I do not reason hypothetically. The case of the patient, on whom Cheselden performed the operation for Cataract, was marked by phenomena which may be adduced as proving the truth of my assertion.

These observations lead us to that part of the subject which is the most intricate and obscure—involving the nature of that reciprocal influence or action which is going on between mind and matter, essential for the manifestation of the former during its earthly condition.

Having assumed that the brain is the seat of mind—that a due and regular supply of blood is essential to the exertion of its faculties—and that dreaming is the result of their imperfect manifestation, it will be right to consider the probable——

CAUSES of a DREAM
*in reference to the intimate function of
the* BRAIN, *and its circulation.*

1. *Predisposing* Cause.— Congestion of
venous or carbonized blood in the vessels
of the brain.

2. *Exciting* Cause.—External or internal
impression on the extremities or origin of
a nerve (of sense ?) at the period of departing or returning consciousness.

3. *Proximate* Cause. — Recurrence of
ideas (erroneously associated).

To the *remote* or *sympathetic* causes,
however, I would previously offer a sepa-
rate but very brief allusion, although they
may at first seem to merit more especial
notice.

The complete consideration of their influence would lead into too wide a field of
discussion. This will be evident, when
I enumerate a part of them. The *supine
position*, intense and undivided *thought*,
repletion, the depression of *fatigue*, the

excitement of *grief* and of *joy,* and the immediate influence of *dyspepsia,* and other varieties of sympathies.

The ancients, among them Galen, attributed dreams chiefly to indigestion, but referred their immediate excitement to fumes and vapours, instead of nervous influence, or cerebral congestion from interrupted circulation.   Herodotus also says, the Atlantes never dream, which Montaigne refers to their never eating any thing which has died of itself; and Burton thus sums up his precepts of prevention :— " Against fearful and troublesome dreams, incubus, and such inconveniences, wherewith melancholy men are molested, the best remedy is, to eat a light supper, and of such meats as are easie of digestion; no hare, venison, beef, &c.—not to lie on his back—not to meditate or think in the day time of any terrible objects, or especially talk of them before he goes to bed."

Indigestion, and that condition which is

termed a weak or irritable stomach, constitute a most fruitful source of dreams.
The immediate or direct influence of repletion, in totally altering the sensations and
the disposition in waking moments, is a
proof of its power to derange the circulation of the brain, and the mental faculties.

The influence of the great sympathetic
nerve in this respect is very important.
With many persons, a meal is usually followed by feelings of depression, and events
will appear of the greatest moment, which
after the lapse of some hours will be considered mere trifles. If the wisdom of life
be contentment, we see how this wisdom
is perverted by repletion. As these sensations have no foundation in reality, we
may almost apply to the train of feelings
induced by dyspepsia, such as abstraction,
impaired memory, unusual timidity, despondency, and other illusive character-
istics of hysteria and hypochondriasis, the
designation of a waking dream.

Mr. Locke informs us, " I once knew a
man who was bred a scholar, and had no
bad memory, who told me, that he had
never dreamed in his life, until he had
fever."

I may merely add, that any influence
which tends to derange or arrest the
upper circulation of blood in its return to
the heart, or which so presses on an important nerve as to disturb the function of
the brain by continuous sympathy, may be
termed the *remote* cause of dreaming.

PREDISPOSING CAUSE.

If, as modern phrenologists, we assume
that there may be distinct portions of the
brain, organs of comparison, individuality,
causality, &c.; we naturally regard them as
the source of that combined faculty which
we denominate Judgment.   We might argue, that if these organs were *permanently*
deficient, fatuity, at least extreme folly,
would be the result: and by parity of rea-

soning, we might infer that, if the function of such organs were for a time suspended, imagination, having lost its mentor, would, as it were, run wild; and an extravagant dream, granting an excitement, would be the result.

Without yielding to the too finely spun hypotheses of Gall, and his whimsical division of the cranium[1], the most frequent coincidence of the possession of great mental power, with full development of the frontal region of the skull, will naturally lead us to believe that it may depend

---

[1] In Dr. Spurzheim's beautiful demonstration of the brain, he exhibits it almost as one large convoluted web. While the ultra-phrenologist is unravelling these convolutions, it is strange that he sees not the inconsistency of his cranial divisions. The boundary lines of his organs are drawn *across* these convolutions.— Should we not rather draw them in the direction of their fibres, for if the faculty be seated in one convolution, that faculty would proceed *in the course* of its fibres, and not across the fissure, from one lobule to another?

E

on causation. As no function, then, either
of brain or gland, can be carried on without
a due supply of blood, it will follow that position may materially influence the integrity
of these functions. The seat of the organs
I have alluded to, if cranial development
supports me, may be determined on the
forepart of the head, behind the os frontis [1],
portions of the cerebral mass, which in the
supine position are usually most elevated
above the centre of circulation; and, con-
sequently, may endure a deficiency of

[1] It is known that very considerable portions of the
cerebrum may be removed, and the individual may still
exist—the vital functions may continue, while the animal functions may be deranged or lost. A patient of
my own, whose skull was fractured, and from whom I
removed a small basin full of cerebrum of the anterior
lobe, survived fifteen days, and died suddenly from
ulceration into the longitudinal sinus, and consequent
venous hæmorrhage. The functions of digestion were
not impaired, there was sensation and volition, a power
to move; the man was at times even cheerful, but the
faculties of correct association, and of memory, were
lost.

stimulus in comparison with other organs more favourably situated [1]. The phrenologist, then, will endeavour to prove that the supine position generally produces vascular pressure on particular parts, or organs of the encephalon; and he will argue that dreams arise from individual organs, abstractedly, or unconnectedly acting. There is one spot on the cranium, indeed, identified by Dr. Spurzheim, as a most important item in the composition of a good dreamer. He tells us, that persons who have the part above, and a little behind the organ of ideality developed, are much prone to mysticism, to see visions, and ghosts, and to dream.

It may not be difficult to believe in this

[1] Blumenbach states that he himself witnessed in one person a sinking of the brain whenever he was asleep, and a swelling with blood when he awoke. And David Hartley imputes dreams to an impediment to the flow of blood, a collapse of the ventricles, and a diminished quantity of their contained serum.

partial function of the brain, when we
recollect how often the loss of one faculty
will be connected with paralytic disorders,
—the faculty of perception may be lost
unless the impression on the mind is made
through a *particular* sense; thus, patients
may be unable to comprehend that name
or subject when it was *pronounced* or related, which he will immediately do if
written down, and presented to his sight;
the optic nerve may transmit, while the
auditory has its power impaired or lost.
On the contrary, there may be the same
imperfection of outward transmission : the
lingual nerves influencing the tongue to
sound a name inapplicable to the idea;
the patient often reversing the names of
articles which he is continually using.
These phenomena, regarding nerves of
sense, then, are strictly analogous to those
which we recognise in those parts of the
brain which are intimately connected with,
or influenced by, these nerves of sense.

The posture of supination will unavoidably induce an increased flow of blood to the brain, which, under certain states of this fluid is so essential to the production of brilliant thoughts; an end, indeed, attained so often by another mode, the swallowing of opium. Some persons always retire to bed when they wish to think, and it is well known that Pope was often wont to ring for pens, ink, and paper in the night, that he might record, ere it was lost, that most sublime or fanciful poesy which flashed through his brain as he lay in bed. I deny not that the darkness or stillness of night may have had some influence during this inspiration: I may also allow that some few individuals compose best while they are walking, but this peripatetic exertion is calculated itself to produce what we term determination of blood to the head. The most remarkable instance of the power of position in influencing mental energy, is that of a German student, who was accustomed to study and compose with his head on the ground, and his feet elevated, and resting against the wall.

It is essential to the perfect function of the brain, the manifestation of mind, not only that it shall have a due supply of blood, but that this blood shall be of that quality we term oxygenated. I have before stated my opinion, in acquiescence with the arguments of Blumenbach, that if there be a simple deficiency of this *scarlet* blood, a state of sound undisturbed sleep will ensue, (an approximation to the condition of syncope.) This may be the consequence of any indirect depression, or the natural indication of that direct debility which we witness in early infancy, and in the "second childishness and mere oblivion" of old age. But the deficiency of arterial blood may be depending on a more positive cause, *venous congestion*, impeding its flow. Even arterial blood itself will become, to a certain degree, carbonized, by lentor or stagnation[1]. We, then, have not only a deficiency of proper stimulus, but a deleterious condition of the blood, which acts as a poison to the brain. Sound sleep is thus prevented, but the congestion of carbonized blood, acting as a sort of narcotic, depresses the energy of the brain, so far as to prevent waking, but induces that middle state, drowsiness or slumber. From this results a dis-

---

[1] Venous congestion and diminution of arterial circulation are not incompatible; indeed, Dr. Abercrombie reasons very ably on their relative nature: implying the necessity of some remora of venous circulation, to supply that want or vacuum, which the brain would otherwise experience from the deficiency of the current in the arterial system. Thus will the languid arterial circulation of the brain, which causes sleep in the first instance, produce, secondarily, that congestion of blood in the veins and sinuses, which shall reduce it to disturbed slumber, and excite the dream. May we not account, on this principle, for the difficulty which many persons experience in falling into a second slumber, when they have been disturbed in the first?

turbed condition of the brain : it is irritated, not excited by its healthy or proper
stimulus, and it follows that such derangement of the manifestations of mind ensues
as we term a dream.

The dream is a slight and transient delirium. Regarding the more permanent
and severe forms of illusion, the unhealthy
crasis of the blood is an important subject
of consideration. Indeed, of itself, it has
been proved the direct cause of furious
and fatal mania. When Dionis, in his
" Cour d' Opérations de Chirurgie," is referring to an operation that has lately, by
its revival, occupied so much of the attention of the medical world, (I mean the
process of transfusion), he says ; " La fin
funeste de ces malheureuses victimes de
la nouveauté detruisit en un jour les
hautes idées qu'ils avoient conçues ; ils
devinrent foux, *furieux* et moururent
ensuite." This analogy will strengthen
the opinion I have advanced, that the

predisposing cause of dreams is the influence of black blood on the brain.

PROXIMATE CAUSE.

Believing that the proximate cause of
the dream consists in a recurrence of ideas
—*memory*—I would consider the

*Origin or mode of impression of a sense,
and the mode of recurrence of such
impression, the* EXCITEMENT *of the
dream.*

It seems to have been the opinion of
Baron Haller, that what we term *impression* of a sense, is, in fact, *mechanical :*
that the rays emanating from a body, and
impinging on the retina, *stamped* an image
on the brain : or, in the words of Aristotle,
" As senses cannot receive material objects, but only their *species*." This idea
regards, also, impression of the other
senses.   Mr. Locke held almost a similar
notion.   The argument involves the cu-

rious physiological question, In what consists the function of a nerve—in oscillation
—in the motion of a fluid—in electricity,
or magnetism ? and, also, that subtle objection which Dr. Reid advanced against
the opinion of Aristotle, and of the more
modern psychologists.

In the absence of a satisfactory answer
to this question, it is certain that external
impressions reach the brain through the
medium of a nerve, and that when the
fibrils, or extremities, of those nerves originally affected, are *again* irritated by their
proper stimulus, and by the same, or a
similar body, an association is produced,
and memory is the result.   Now I cannot
think but that this principle obtains, both
in a waking thought, and in a dream.   I
have asserted that as the mind is gradually
approaching the condition of sleep, or re-
covering from it, there is a state produced
more or less approximating the more simple animal life, in which certain faculties

may be perceived, but in which the power
of correct association is not manifested.
There is a curious calculation of Cabanis,
that certain parts or senses of the body
fall asleep at regular progressive periods;
I can readily carry on this analogy to the
faculties of mind. We may suppose that
the faculty of judgment, as being the most
important, is the first to feel fatigue, and
to be influenced in the mode I have alluded to, by slumber. It is evident, then,
that the other faculties which are still
awake, will be uncontrolled, and an imperfect association will be the result, es-
tablishing the axiom I have ventured to
advance. It is essential, however, that
some object, or subject, be presented to
the faculty of perception, ere this recurrence can take place. A sound, a touch, an
odour, or a ray of light, may influence the
sense and the brain: the idea, or thought,
that had lain dormant will then be re-
excited by that mysterious sympathy of

brain and nerve, and it will traverse the track of nerve from its origin to its fibrillous expansion on the organ of sense, or the spot at which the original impression was received, the only spot on which it can be re-excited.

These reminiscences will occur sometimes in the most sudden and unexpected manner. In one of the American Journals we are told of a clergyman, who, at the termination of some depressing malady, had completely lost his memory. His mind was a blank, and he had, in fact, to begin the world of literature again. Among other of his studies was the Latin language. During his classical readings with his brother, he one day suddenly struck his head with his hand, and stated that he had a most *peculiar feeling*, and was convinced that he had learned all this before.

Boerhaave, in his Prelectiones Academic. Institut. Med., relates the case of a Spanish tragic writer, whose memory, subsequently to an acute febrile disease, was so completely impaired, that not only the literature of various languages he had studied was lost to him, but also their elements, the alphabets. When even his own poetic compositions were read to him, he denied himself to be the author. But the most interesting feature of the case is this, that on becoming *again* a votary of the muse, his recent compositions so intimately resembled his original productions in style and sentiment, that he no longer doubted that both were the offspring of his own imagination.

Another instance is that of the Countess of Laval, who had apparently forgotten the language of the Welch, among whom a portion of her childhood had been passed. After she had attained the adult age she had a fever, and during her delirium she again spoke Welch fluently. We are informed by Thucydides, that in many of

those who survived the plague in Athens,
the recollection of the names of their
friends and themselves was for a time
quite gone.   It returned as health became
more established.

But the faculty of memory may be impaired only from one certain period: the
impressions previous to that time only
being capable of renewal.   In the case
related by Dr. Abercrombie, of a lady
reduced by diarrhœa, the memory of ten
years was lost.   " Her ideas were consistent with each other, but they referred
to things as they stood before her removal
(to Edinburgh)."   In these instances it is
probable that the fault may be referred to
the *original* impression, some disorder or
state of the brain causing it to be only
superficially impressed during these ten
years.   It does not, I believe, require *ex-*
ternal impression of sense always to produce this excitement.   We know that
local congestions at the origin of nerves

of sense will influence its condition, so as
to render it additionally acute, or to destroy
it altogether; and it is not impossible but
that impression or excitement on that spot
of brain on which the original image
rested, may occasion this recurrence of
ideas—memory.

That the possession of the faculty of
this *impression* of memory can be demonstrated, we might doubt, were verbal description only employed; but when we see
the artist trace the features of a person
long lost to us, from memory, we know
that such ideas existed, and were then re-
excited in his mind.

That curious fact, the reference of pain
to a toe or finger, after the amputation of the
limb to which they belonged, is the effect of
this memory. The impression of pain has
been conveyed from the extreme fibrillæ of
the nerve to the brain. If, then, subsequent to amputation, any part of the re-
mainder of that nerve be irritated or

touched, the impression will be revived in the sensorium, and the erroneous sensation will for a time occur.

The original impressions in all cases are from without. It may be asked, then, how the excited idea is presented as a prominent image *before* the eye?

That form of disordered vision termed *muscæ volitantes,* which occurs so often in nervous persons, or is the result of close application to study, does not often appear to depend on a turgid condition of the vessels of the choroid or retina. It is usually relieved more by tonics than by depletion, and very strange illusions of sight will sometimes be produced by depressing medicines, especially the preparations of antimony. Yet these dark specks appear to be floating *before* the retina, and often at some distance withoutside the eye; therefore, we may believe that excited images, or more perfect forms may appear before the retina, palpable. Between the first impression and its recurrence, a long period may have passed, memory being unlimited ; and it is sufficient that one sole idea be excited to produce a succession, as a spark of fire will ignite a train of gunpowder; or as an electric spark will discharge a whole battery.

It has been asked how, if the particles of the body are constantly changing, memory can exist in the brain ; the answer is easy, because particles of exact similarity are deposited as others are removed. The parts thus regenerated, whether muscle, gland, nerve, or brain, still being identical and unchanged in function: this reasoning may at first appear to invalidate the *substantial impression* of Haller, but the atomic theory will probably afford a fair explanation of his views. I have thus endeavoured to explain the excitement of latent ideas, or memory ; but we may suppose that the period of slumber may have

F

been so limited that the subject on which
the mind had been reflecting, shall have
scarcely disappeared from it, the thought
has not had time to cool—

"Lateat scintillula forsan;"

the slightest disturbance, then, of whatever
nature, will be sufficient to revive the original train of thought.

In the arguments I have adduced, I
have referred chiefly to the *imperfect*
associations of a dream. Slumbering
visions, are, however, it must be allowed,
often marked by a very great degree of
consistency, especially when they refer to
an occurrence or action of recent date.
If even these rational dreams be carefully
related, and as carefully considered, it
will usually be found that, though consistent in a general bearing, the details
may yet be in some degree imperfect.

It is rational to suppose that the idea
last imprinted on the mind, or which had

more exclusively occupied its powers, would be the first to influence, as the mental manifestations were awakened ere the image of fresh objects had been perceived. To this cause we may probably refer the facility with which a school lesson, conned over even slightly on the previous night, is recollected by the student on awaking the next morning.

This is the language of Claudian on the subject :—

" Omnia quæ sensu volvuntur vota diurno
Pectore sopito reddit amica quies.
Venator defessa toro cum membra reponit
Mens tamen ad sylvas et sua lustra redit [1]."

And in the Anatomie of Melancholy, we have the following quaint summary :

[1] All the wishes of the day appear to be realised in sleep. When the hunter flings his weary limbs on the couch, his fancy still wanders to the woods and the dens of wild animals.

" As Tully notes, ' for the most part our
speeches in the day time cause our phan-
tasy to work upon the like in our sleep,'
which Ennius writes of Homer,

' Et Canis in somnis leporis vestigia latrat ;'

as a dog dreams of a hare, so do men on
such subjects they thought on last.

' Somnia quæ mentes ludunt volitantibus umbris,
Nec delubra deûm nec ab æthere numina mittunt.
Sed sibi quisque facit,' &c.

" For that cause, when Ptolemy, king
of Egypt, had posed the seventy interpre-
ters in order, and asked the nineteenth
man what would make one sleep quietly
in the night, he told him, ' the best way
was to have divine and celestial medita-
tions, and to use honest actions in the
day time.'   Lod. Oives wonders how
Schoolmen could sleep quietly, and were
not terrified in the night, they had such
monstrous questions, and thought of such

terrible matters all day long! They had
need, amongst the rest, to sacrifice to god
Morpheus, whom Philostratus paints in
a white and black coat, with a horn and
ivory box full of dreams of the same
colours, to signify good and bad."

With the relations and illustrations of
these good and bad dreams, the pages of
both fiction and authentic history abound.
Lucia exclaims :

> " Sweet are the slumbers of the virtuous man,
>   Oh Marcia ! I have seen thy godlike father,
>   Some power invisible supports his soul,
>   And bears it up in all its wonted greatness.
>   A kind refreshing sleep is fallen upon him,
>   I saw him stretched at ease, his fancy lost
>   In pleasing dreams : I drew near his couch,
>   He smiled, and cried, 'Cæsar, thou can'st not
>   hurt me !' "

While the coward conscience of Richard
thus speaks :

> " By the apostle Paul, shadows to-night
>   Have struck more terror to the soul of Richard
>   Than could the substance of ten thousand soldiers."

The records of national and domestic history, the dreams of the conqueror of thousands, and of the midnight assassin, are replete with illustrations.

As the arguments of Tertullian, and the notion of a special purpose of the Deity in the excitement of a dream, are entertained so generally, it will be right, perhaps, to consider this point, to enquire into the *cui bono* of our visions. *In limine,* I assert my belief that the days of special inspiration are past, and that we cannot, rationally, now regard the visions of slumber as revelations or prognostics. Indeed, when we reflect that the proportion of those events which may seem even to have been the fulfilment of a dream, are to those myriads of visionary prophecies which never come to pass as a drop in the ocean, the fallacy of this doctrine must be evident. It is true, that there appears in some dreams a remarkable coincidence with subsequent events, but these are, indeed,

"Like angels' visits, few and far between;"

and do not disprove, nay, rather prove my
opinion by the exceptions. The fulfilment is a *coincidence,* and not a consequence. If dreams are prophetic, why
are they not *all* fulfilled? reasoning *à
priori,* if one is not fulfilled, how know
we if all will not be equally fallacious?
The argument for the prophetic nature of
dreams is merely *à posteriori;* it is the
shallow *post hoc ergo propter hoc* of the
sophist. On the occurrence of any important event, all the auguries and dreams
which bear the slightest semblance to a
prophecy, are immediately brought forward, and stretched, and warped, to suit
the superstition; as the whimsical mother
will decide on the exciting causes of the
marks, redundancies, and deficiencies of
her child, by frights, by longings, and the
like.

The prophetic warnings of Lord Lyttleton, and others, may be more than

impressive, they may be convincing to the
unreflecting mind, but when we know that
myriads of enthusiasts, or hypochondriacs,
have, by the failure of their prognostics,
deserved the stigma of false prophets,
we may surely class these fantasies among
the popular errors of the time. Some
imputation of suicidal disposition has been
lately thrown on Lord Lyttleton. This, if
substantiated, will wholly invalidate the
prophetic nature of this story. These
superstitious notions ought not to be en-
couraged, since apprehension of a misfortune, or fatality, may prove its cause.
We should rather echo the benevolent
precept of Horace :

" Tu ne quæsieris (scire nefas) quem mihi, quem tibi,
   Finem Dii dederint, Leuconöe [1]."

The dream and death of Glaphyra are an
illustration of this melancholy influence.
She " was married while she was a virgin

[1] " Seek not to know the destiny which awaits us."

to Alexander, the son of Herod, and brother
of Archelaus; but since it fell out so that
Alexander was slain by his father, she was
married to Juba, the king of Lydia; and
when he was dead, and she lived in
widowhood in Cappadocia with her father, Archelaus divorced his former wife
Mariamne, and married her, so great was
his affection for this Glaphyra; who during
her marriage to him saw the following
dream. She thought ' she saw Alexander
standing by her, at which she rejoiced,
and embraced him, with great affection;
but that he complained of her, and said,
O Glaphyra, thou provest that saying to
be true, which assures us that women are
not to be trusted. Didst not thou pledge
thy faith to me? and wast thou not married to me when thou wast a virgin? and
had we not children between us? Yet
hast thou forgotten the affection I bare to
thee, out of a desire of a second husband.

Nor hast thou been satisfied with that
injury thou didst me, but thou hast been
so bold as to procure thee a third husband,
and hast been married to Archelaus thy
husband, and my brother. However, I
will not forget my former affection for thee,
but will set thee free from every such re-
proachful action, and cause thee to be
mine again as thou once wast.' When
she had related this to her female companions in a few days' time she departed
this life."—*Josephus' Ant. of Jews.*

I believe that many modern instances
of gradual, and almost imperceptible decay, may be referred to the influence of
melancholy visions on the mind, although
this agency may be as obscure as that of
the *aqua tofana* of the *Italians.*

The most interesting history of the sublime Requiem of Mozart, although not the
recital of a dream, except that we might
call the consequent train of thought of the

composer, intense as it was, by that name, is highly illustrative of the influence of melancholy and sombre impressions in the production of a fatal result.

In the æras of inspiration few will be sceptical enough to doubt the occurrence of divine mediations during the silence of a dream, or deep sleep : or not to believe with Socrates, and other sages, in the divine origin of dreams and omens. Although Socrates himself, however, believed and asserted that he was controlled in his actions by a familiar demon, it is the more rational opinion of some of his commentators, that this invisible monitor was merely the impersonation of the faculty of judgment, and of that extensive knowledge and fore-thought with which his mind was fraught. The evidence of Holy Scripture proves the occasion, indeed, the necessity for such communication; but in our own time, I should deem it little less than profaneness to imagine that the Deity should

indicate the future occurrence of common-
place and trivial incidents through the
medium of an organ confessedly in a state
of *imperfection*, at the moment when the
faculties of mind are returning from a
state of temporary suspension—a death-
like sleep.

Among those heathen tribes where this
sentiment forms part of a national creed,
we perceive it marked by a degree of
blindness and inconsistency that may truly
be termed mania : it is the doctrine not of
prophecy, but of debased and absolute
fatalism.   The North-American Indians
not only regard the dream as prophetic,
but often receive it as a solemn injunction,
and are themselves the active agents in its
fulfilment.   " In whatever manner," says
Charlevoix, " the dream is conceived, it is
always looked upon as a thing sacred, and
as the most ordinary way in which the
gods make known their will to men. Filled
with this idea, they cannot conceive how

we should pay no regard to them. For
the most part they look upon them either
as a desire of the soul, inspired by some
genius, or an order from him, and in consequence of this principle, they hold it a
religious duty to obey them. An Indian
having dreamt of having a finger cut off,
had it really cut off as soon as he awoke,
having first prepared himself for this important action by a feast."

Dreams may, however, be instructive
lessons as well as some waking reflections,
and others may indeed be so far prophetic,
that persons may be induced to action from
their impression, the consequences of this
action being the fulfilment of a prophecy.
The dream of Olympia, for instance, that
she was with child of a dragon, might
both have suggested the mode of education, and incited the warlike spirit of
Alexander. On this principle of an imparted impetus, or motive of action, in
conjunction with confidence and faith, may

perhaps be explained, the excitement of *chorea simulata*, or *tarantism*; the miracles of Hohenloe; the charm of *amulets* and *talismans;* the fulfilment of *omens,* and of *oracles;* and the wisdom of *astrology*, of *chiromancy*, and the *horoscope.*

The prophetic dream of Cromwell, that he should be the greatest man in England, is emphatically adduced as a proof of Divine fore-knowledge imparted to the mind of man. But the ambitious thoughts of this man were constantly haunting his waking moments, pointing to personal aggrandizement : it follows that this constant dwelling on the subject must have imparted a like character to the dream of his slumbers. But could we have penetrated the privacy of Ireton, of Lambert, or other presbyterian rebels, we should, doubtless, discover that such ambitious prepossessions were not confined to the bosom of the Protector. A similar explanation will apply to the dream of the Emperor Julian,—to the fabulous vision of Calpurnia,—the dream of Morton, related by Defoe, and others.

The intense feelings and influence of conscience and remorse, in regard to the excitement of dreaming, are so notorious as to require no argument or examples as a proof.

SOMNAMBULISM.

———

Doct. You see her eyes are open.
Gent. Aye, but their sense is shut.

MACBETH.

THERE are certain phenomena closely
allied to those of dreaming, which are yet
of so rare occurrence that we must conclude
some difference in their immediate causes.
It appears that the somnambulist differs
from the common dreamer in the relative
possession of *sensation* or *consciousness*
and *volition*, and in the eccentricity of
nervous transmission.   In reasoning on
sensation and volition we believe that the
excitement of the first is from external—
of the second, from internal impression.
In the condition of somnambulism this
property, sensation, seems often to be

totally suspended, and it is usually so far
weakened that external contact does not
produce that mental consciousness which
is calculated to excite alarm. It appears
to be an intense degree of mental abstraction, and is evidently a nearer approach to
the state of waking than what we commonly denominate a dream.

The evidence of volition is peculiarly
forcible in the expansion of the eye-lids.
Vision is the only sense, the organ of
which is mechanically closed against its
proper stimulus during sleep.   Light only
is certainly not the cause of this shutting,
as the lid equally precludes the admission
of its rays as during sleep ; and if a candle
be held to the eye of the somnambulist,
there will be the actions of the iris visible,
but no aversion of the head to avoid the
glare.   It must be on this point, then, to
the *sensorium,* and not the *sense,* that we
would refer the disorder.

G

Although the actions of somnambulists appear almost automatic, it is evident that they have some determinate motive for them, a conviction of necessity which arose while they were awake. They have generally been thinking much ere they retire to rest; and the walk occurs usually so early in the night, that we might sometimes doubt if a mood of musing had not actually prevented sleep, and itself been the cause of the phenomena.

The actions performed, unlike the ideas of a dream, are often far from being heterogeneous or inconsistent; they are usually what the sleep-walker has been engaged in while awake, and it is astonishing to observe the exactness and perfection with which the work is executed, and if we could reconcile our notions to the seeming paradox of a will without consciousness, we might conclude that it is owing to that abstraction of mind in which its ener-

9

gies are directed to one sole object. The
faculties of association and comparison cannot be dormant—though judgment cannot
altogether have slept—but these faculties
are as it were like rays converging to one
point. This peculiar feature bears a close
analogy to that form of insanity—the reverse of monomania, in which there is an
aberration of intellect or a want of consciousness, on all subjects but one. Of
this form of derangement we have not infrequent examples. I believe some portions of a great national establishment for
lunatics, were constructed from the plans
of one of its unfortunate inmates, who, although his genius and his science were
then so perfect on the subject of architec-
ture, as to create designs of great brilliancy, was to all other intents and pur-
poses, insane.

Other instances of this curious form of
insanity, this " follie raisonnante," may be

G 2

cited—for instance, that of an insane musical professor, whose musical talents were
increased in the ratio of his general derangement; and that of a clergyman who
was ever insane but when he was deli-
vering his discourses from the pulpit.

The weakened power of judgment is
proved by the want of reflection in the
somnambulist, in case of obstruction to
his apparent intentions; under these im-
pediments the sleep-walker has been known
to cry. In other instances, on the contrary, there is added to the consciousness
of obstruction, an excessive, and almost
preternatural desire and power of resist-
ance: so firm is the patient's conviction
of the necessity of his performing some
act or duty. This was exemplified in the
following case, attended about eight years
ago, by a gentleman in Westminster-road;
which, however, was not one of genuine
somnambulism, but rather of transient

delirium, from plethora of the cerebral vessels :—still the analogy to somnambulism is not remote.

A butcher's boy, about sixteen years old, apparently in perfect health, after dosing a few minutes in his chair, suddenly started up, and began to employ himself about his usual avocations. Having saddled and mounted his horse, it was with the greatest difficulty that those around him could remove him from the saddle, and carry him within doors. While he was held in the chair by force, he continued violently the actions of kicking, whipping, and spurring. His observations regarding orders from his master's customers, the payment at the turnpike-gate, &c. were seemingly rational. The eyes, when opened, were perfectly sensible to light. It appears that flagellation even had no effect in restoring the patient to a proper sense of his condition. The pulse in this case was 130, full and hard—on the ab-

straction of 30 oz. of blood it shrunk to 80,
and diaphoresis ensued. After labouring
under this phrenzy for the space of an
hour, he became sensible—was astonished
at what he was told had happened, and
stated that he recollected nothing, subsequent to his having fetched some water,
and moved from one chair to another,
which he had done immediately before his
delirium came on.

The sleep-walker will often recall some
determination to rise early for some purpose or occupation, and we may suppose
that this feeling influences the mind at the
period of commencing sleep, when the
judgment neither recognises time nor
space. The memory, at a certain point of
this slumber, is excited, and the action is
that of an automaton, the dreamer returning to bed unconscious of having performed
it, and astonished to find it so performed
the next morning, and what is equally
strange, without the sensation of pain or

fatigue, although the occupation may have
been one of a laborious nature.

> " A great perturbation in nature,
>   To receive at once the benefit of sleep,
>   And do the effects of watching !"

Somewhat analogous to this is the ease
and activity with which, we are told, some
mental operations have been conducted
during sleep, which have produced great
pain and uneasiness, if performed during
waking moments.

If the dreamer be awakened, he will relate the circumstances of his dream usually
clearly ; but if the somnambulist be roused
at the commencement or end of his walking, he will generally express himself unconscious of what he intended to do, or of
what he had done.

The very close resemblance which the
movements of some somnambulists bear to
the symptoms of chorea and other spasmodic diseases, offer some analogical aid in

the explanation of the causes of sleep-
walking. Although dissection has not
yet elucidated the point, in some cases of
periodical chorea the paroxysms have un-
usually come on during the sleep of the
patient. In the northern districts of Scotland, a most eccentric form of the disease
is not infrequent, which is vulgarly termed
" leaping ague." The patients, when the
fit is on them, " run with astonishing velocity, and often over dangerous passes,
to some place out of doors which they have
fixed on in their own minds, or, perhaps,
even mentioned to those in company with
them, and then drop down quite exhausted.
At other times, especially when confined
to the house, they climb in the most sin-
gular manner. In cottages, for example,
they leap from the floor to what are called
the baulks, or those beams by which the
rafters are joined together, springing from
one to the other with the agility of a cat,

or whirling round one of them with a motion resembling the fly of a jack." *Ed. M. & S. Jour.* vol. iii.

I have quoted enough to shew how much the somnambulist resembles these patients, in that almost preternatural triumph over the infirmities of nature by which they may seem to subvert the laws of gravitation and the principles of mechanics. In other cases, the sound of drums, &c. seem to act as an excitement to the paroxysms, resembling the influence which produces those effects before alluded to in regard to Tarantism, and animal magnetism. A not infrequent connection has also been observed between the disease epilepsy and somnambulism. Epileptic idiots especially, are peculiarly prone to walk in their sleep: and I have remarked, that in these, there appears, as in chorea, to be a sort of *imitatire* propensity, analogous to that delirium which came upon so many of the Abderites, on witnessing the performance of the Andromeda of Euripides by Archelaus. It is not visionary, moreover, to believe that there is some resemblance between that sensation termed *aura epileptica*, and the sensations which may excite somnambulism, arising from some primary irritation of the brain, imparting an erroneous reflex feeling of impression.

There is a disease in sheep, arising from hydatids within the brain, symptoms of which resemble both epilepsy and chorea, and in which the motions of the animal assume sometimes the unconscious aspect of somnambulism.

The diseases I have mentioned, it is true, occur at uncertain intervals, and usually during waking moments; somnambulism requires the superadded cause of slumber. In all, however, we discern some peculiar condition of mental faculties

with which voluntary motion is associated.
We believe that there may be certain
vessels which contribute to nervous energy,
or as some have conceived, secrete the
nervous fluid in the brain. It is probable,
that this nervous influence has often been
secreted, if I may so express it, while
the person was awake; or, in other
words, the resolution to act has been
formed : when the faculty of judgment is
asleep, this impression becomes uncontrolled, and the night-walk takes place.
There may be also an *excess* of this nervous energy—or the principle by which
muscular action is excited or supported—
by undue exertion, this may be as speedily
exhausted as it is formed—if, then, during
sleep, there is a reproduction of this excessive energy, the motive powers of the
body are naturally and forcibly stimulated
to action. The somnambulist, then, requires this state of repose; and it is highly
probable, that, if previous to sleep, he

were to employ powerful exertion, the walk
would not take place.

The predisposing cause of somnambulism
must still be involved in obscurity. It is
the diversified conditions of the brains of
maniacs, which render it so difficult to reason on the predisposing cause of insanity.
In almost all cases, however, some portion of the brain is diseased. In epilepsy,
especially that form occurring in maniacs
and idiots, we shall usually discover either
effusion, congestion, membranous ossifi-
cation, ramollissement, or bony spiculæ.
In the cases of epileptic sleep-walkers,
almost every portion of the brain has been
occasionally found diseased. A thickened
or ossified condition of portions of the
pia mater or arachnoid, a shrunk state of
the testes of the brain, indurcissement or
ramollissement, and tubercles or cysts, developed in the substance of the brain. In
some, the cranium has assumed the density
of ivory. This condition may, perhaps,

induce congestion by diminishing the fora-
mina, and impeding the return of venous
blood from the brain.

The want of uniformity in the appear-
ances on examination of patients simply
known to be sleep-walkers, is at present
discouraging. In chorea very frequently,
and in the somnambulist, we have ascer-
tained that, previous to the dance or the
night walk, pain has been felt about the
occiput, and in the course of the upper
portion of the spinal marrow. In other
cases, chorea will be produced during
slumber by some agitating cause, or violent
motion on the previous day. Patients are,
from these causes, sometimes seized in
bed with an irresistible rolling motion,
and their actions, on such occasions, very
closely resemble somnambulism [1]. Al-

[1] In future dissections it would be well that we
should pay particular attention to the arachnoid of the
brain and spinal chord, and also to those parts in the
vicinity of the medulla oblongata, where pain is often

though pain in the abdomen is seldom
complained of in any of these diseases,
yet there appears to be, from the influence
which dyspepsia and other abdominal derangements exert over them, some peculiar
sympathy excited between the ganglionic
system, or the nerves of organic life and
the brain, previous to the attacks. We
cannot, at present, be prepared to impute
the excitement of somnambulism always
to diseased structure. I believe that conditions of much less importance will be
sufficient to produce it where there is that
peculiar irritability and tendency of mind.

The arguments I have adduced on the
subject of venous congestion regarding the
dream, with some modification, would

complained of previous to the paroxysms—such dissection may illustrate an analogous fact, that soldiers struck
by a ball about the cervical vertebræ, often spring from
the ground and drop dead; and it would also, perhaps,
establish the opinion of Flourens, that the cerebellum
is influential over the progressive or *forward* motions
of animals.

apply to the present subject; a peculiar
disposition to be acted on by certain
causes, being, moreover, inherent in the
nervous apparatus of the motive powers.

REVERIE.

My Lord is often thus—
The fit is momentary, upon a thought
He will again be well.

MACBETH.

As somnambulism appears to be the
slightest condition of sleep, there is an
easy transition to that state which presents the nearest approximation to slumber, and which we understand by the
terms reverie, abstraction, day-dream, or
absent fit. Perhaps, as I profess the consideration of imperfect manifestations of
mind, I should commence with this subject in its lowest and most derogatory
form, in which individuals in an absent

mood commit the most absurd acts, and utter the most ridiculous expressions, without the redeeming apology of being engaged in abstract contemplation, or abstruse calculations. It is sufficient, however, merely to allude to this weakness, which indicates a want of power generally in the faculties of the mind ; it is indeed that slight form of idiotism or fatuity, on which have been founded the plot and incidents of many a stage farce : and closely allied to it is that strange mixture of weakness and cunning which is delineated in Davie Gellatly, and the absolute imbecility of Audrey, Slender, and Sir Andrew Aguecheek.

We may, however, chance to have witnessed that degree of abstraction approaching to the state of night-walking, in which a person has been engaged about something which he may be ignorant of having done, and have had no motive for doing

H

In the day-dream, a thought or form
shall present itself, even at a time when
the mind is employed on subjects of a contrasted nature. These thoughts or forms
are usually fraught with a high degree of
pleasure or of pain, or refer to events of
vital importance to the dreamer: such are
the objects of the lover's idolatry, and
subjects of prospective felicity. Under
this excitement the influence of external
objects is often for a time lost—the *retina*
may be struck by a ray, or the *membrana
tympani* by a vibration, but the mind
shall fail in its perception, no internal impression being made. This cannot arise
from a point of the retina, or of the expansion of the auditory nerve being pre-
occupied, as some have supposed: the
idea of material impression must fail in
its explanation, for on the instant that the
mind is awakened, the external impression is again perceived. The external
sense in this case is not in fault; nor is its

direct influence on the sensorium suspended; for we find that a person will
continue to read in this state, as it were,
mechanically, but the attention of the
mind is diverted by deep thought, so that
the reader, at the end of his task, may
have no remembrance of what he has been
reading.

Another species of reverie is that which
is induced by moroseness,—the depression of disease itself, or the occurrence of
misfortune. This 'brown study' is the characteristic of morbid sensibility of a mind
easily influenced by the minutiæ of existence. Its slightest form is that state
which the French have termed *ennui*; its
more severe symptoms are those of misan-
thropy, melancholy, and hypochondriasis,
inducing, in some instances, that *tædium
vitæ*, the climax of which is suicide.

The reverie is not, however, always
confined to one subject; it may consist of
a wandering of the imaginative faculty of

H 2

mind,—of a train of ideas, between the
links of which there is an intimate rela-
tion, but its beginning and end may appear so dissonant, that the absent person
himself may fail to recognize the connection, until, by an effort of recollection, he
is induced to retrace the steps of thought,
and in this way the mystery is developed.
Of this nature is the case, related by
Bossuet, of one who, when quite awake,
often saw landscapes and figures as
plainly as if they were real.   During this
influence, we may often find that the features or corporeal actions shall prove an
involuntary, though correct index of the
thought.   According to the passions or
subjects which occupy the mind, will be
the play of feature, or the movement of
the body.

"We might almost suppose the body thought."

To this species is intimately allied the
inspiration of poetical fancy.

The *train* of ideas is peculiarly expressive of this form of reverie, as also of the dream; and the works of the painters who have illustrated the fantasia of themselves or others, often represent something of this regular series of objects. I would offer as an instance, the sketch of the dream of Queen Catherine of Arragon, by Blake,—a legion of spirits, who seem to emanate from the celestial abode, and to descend, in a waving line, until they may surround the person of the dreamer.

When we are roaming over the flowery fields of poesy, we are seldom inclined to reflect on the mental labour by which they are embellished. We may suppose, that, whatever is born of the brain is ushered in by an easy birth; but poesy is often attended by a pang of parturition, and one single line may rankle in the brain for hours ere it struggles into light, and, perhaps, require a frontal blow, as

violent as that which cleft the skull of Ju-
piter and gave birth to Pallas.

There are some minds which can support the effort of composition with impu-
nity ; but when we recollect the diseases
which are entailed on genius, the melancholy of Cowper, and the distraction of
the amiable Collins [1] ; when we are told
that Ariosto was never seen to laugh, and
rarely to smile ; and when we reflect on
the premature decay of unhappy White—

When science self destroy'd her fav'rite son !

we are not only led to confess, that the
flight of fancy is an effort of illusion, but

[1] Though nature gave him, and though science taught,
  The fire of fancy and the reach of thought,
  Severely doom'd to penury's extreme,
  He passed in madd'ning pain life's fev'rish dream.
  While rays of genius only serv'd to show
  The thick'ning horror and exalt his woe.

        *Inscription by Hayley, on Collins's Monument, at
        Chichester.*

almost echo the apostrophe of Words-
worth—

We poets in our youth begin in gladness,
But thereof comes in the end, despondency and
    madness !

The natural brilliancy of thought may
be imitated too by the swallowing of
opium; but the use of this narcotic is as
sure a poison as intensity of thought; but
the one, as it is a part of our being, we
can only control, and that effort is painful; but when we consider the consequences of undue excitement by the narcotic, the moral delinquency of the practised opium-eater seems little less than
madness.

The visions of the opium-eater are, indeed, a modification of delirium, and, under its influence, the master passions of
the individual are intensely developed in
his actions and his writings. This effect
is somewhat analogous to that of *nitrous*

oxyde inhalation, in a degree less intense, perhaps, but for a period far more protracted.

The poem of " Kubla Khan," which Coleridge has termed a psychological curiosity (why, I know not), had its origin in the excitement of opium,—an effort of the characteristic imagination of the poet, consisting in the recurrence of the wild images which had been before presented to the mind's eye of the enthusiast. They are, indeed, but impressions of the pleasures and the pains of memory.

During the reverie of the opium-eater, (I do not mean the deep sleep produced by a full dose, but the first and second stages, ere *coma* be induced,) he is, indeed, a poet, so far as vivid imagination is concerned, but his scribbling would be mere " midsummer madness,"—the evidences of intoxication, of that effect which is closely analogous to the illusions produced by those vapours and gases which

are so essential in the spells and incantations of the magician : the disengagement
of the volatile parts or properties, in
which consist the virtues of certain vege-
table narcotics. But the philosophy,
the metaphysics of poetry, are not the product of mere excitement,—"*poeta nasci-
tur, non fit !*"

The influence of opium, also, on the
philosopher, or the orator, is the same, but
in them it does not usually elevate the
faculty of imagination beyond that of
judgment. The power of the faculties
has been, in fact, exhausted by thought or
study. The stimulus of opium, then, re-
stores that depressed energy to its proper
level, leaving the judgment perfect and
not overbalanced. So that the excitement be obtained, it, perhaps, matters not
how ; whether by the use of opium, as in
the case of some of our modern statesmen,
or the free libation of brandy, in certain
departed orators, who were wont to stag-

ger down to the House from White's, with
those club-house laurels, wet towels, round
their brows, and overwhelm St. Stephen's
by the thunders of their eloquence [1].

The power of abstracting and fixing the
attention on one subject is the great characteristic of the philosopher, especially of
the mathematician, and may be held as one
form of reverie.   It is sometimes termed
strength of mind ; notwithstanding the in-
attention to minutiæ, during this abstraction, has caused the shafts of satire to be
profusely flung at many a learned pundit.
So intense, indeed, has sometimes been
its influence, that Pliny contemplated the
volcanic philosophy amid the dense ashy
cloud of Vesuvius, by which he was at
length destroyed ; and Archimedes was
so intent in solving a problem, during the

[1] The seeds of stramonium, if swallowed by children,
will produce a sort of temporary delirium, or a state
approaching chorea,—singing, dancing, laughing, and
other mad frolics, which cannot be controlled.

siege of Syracuse, that no sense of danger
impelled him to avoid the storm, or to
fly from the dagger of the assassin.

In the case of Archimedes, it is clear
that the deep interest of the subject on
which he was reflecting overbalanced the
influence of the *external* senses, through
which the impression of objects was
therefore too slight or rapid to impress
the mind, and excite perception ; for an
adequate force or a sufficient space of
time must be granted ere the mind shall
be made perfectly conscious of an object
presented to it.

These abstract moods have, I am convinced, been often confounded with the
visions of slumber, and have been adduced as proofs of the perfection of mind
during sleep ; thus, when we are told of
a person, who when asleep, could be made
to dream on any given subject, by merely
talking to him to that effect, I believe this
mistake is made. When we are told, also,

of the brilliant parody composed by Mac-
kenzie—of the solution of the difficult problem by Condorcet, during an actual dream,
it is evident to us that these celebrated
men were not then overcome by sleep,
but merely in that state we term reverie.
In this intermediate state, the faculties
of perception being, as it were, suspended,
one only subject occupies the mind :
hence the vivid and permanent impression
on the judgment, and also on the imagination, of which the most interesting
illustration is the dream, as it is termed,
of Tartini, and its exquisite product—" La
Sonata di Diavolo."

The action of mind is thus concen-
trated, and, if I may so express it, works
with more ease, and greater activity, because there is no object to impede its
unity, by calling off its attention ; or in
the phraseology of Stewart, " because the
mental conception of slumber is uninfluenced by conscious perception."

This effect is, in a slight degree, produced by excluding rays of light from the
retina. The common mode of fixing the
thought is by shutting the eyes. Thus, in
fact, may the pleasing dream be for some
seconds actually prolonged; of which we
have a poetical illustration in the Canzone
of Sanazzaro.

To this result we have some analogy in
the acuteness and power which are added
to one sense on the failure of another.
For instance, the fineness of ear, and the
delicacy of touch possessed by the blind,
as illustrated by the cases of Miss M'Avoy,
of the late Mr. Stanley the organist, of
Professor Sanderson, and others :—and the
astonishing perfection of memory in the
instance of the blind girl, related by Mr.
Mouchart in the Psychological Magazine.
On this principle, too, we may account
for the

" Ruling passion strong in death,"

when every other idea had ceased to influence [1].

It is on this account, too, that the excitement of terror which had taken full possession of the mind by the aid of wild imagination in the dark, is lessened by any sound or sight which presents an object to the faculty of perception. For instance, the sudden glimmer of a light, or the barking of a dog, or the almost instinctive effort of the schoolboy,

" Whistling aloud to keep his courage up."

---

[1] The right hand of Benjamin West, of which I saw a model at Lord de Tabley's, appeared to have taken that form in which it was wont to hold the pencil ; whether this was a convulsive action in muscles constantly so exerted, or the indication of this solemn and last reverie, I leave to others to determine.

SPECTRAL ILLUSION.

———————————

—————————————"A false creation,
Proceeding from the heat oppressed brain."
                                    MACBETH.

IN most of the historical traditions of
Spectral Illusion, those which are authenticated as having been seen by an individual, the phantom has possessed the
form of some person, or is endued with
some shape or properties relating to *former*
impressions on the mind, in which they
have been called up. Personal visions of
this sort are of course those only in which
we can place credence, referring them, as
we must do, to substantial causes. There
are, of course, many spectral visions,

where no previous impression can be distinctly traced; where merely a vague remembrance of the illusion is existing in the mind. This arises from a *faintness* of the impression, common to dreaming and to waking. The recital of such visions will, of course, be very indefinite; resembling the description which Johnson gives of the ghost which appeared to old Cave—"Sir, something of a shadowy being."

Such as are reported to have appeared to a multitude, we must deem imposture; yet to these general visitations, even Pliny the consul is inclined to give credence. In his Letter to Sura concerning Spectres, he alludes with much seriousness to the vision of Curtius Rufus, and to the haunted house of Athenodorus. These, however, are marked by little more plausibility than the Hammersmith and Cock Lane phantoms, or those creations which are so profusely scattered over the pages of fiction.

I allude to the familiar spirits of the ancients, the superstitions of Runic, or Cel-
tic, of oriental or transatlantic mythology,
and the mysteries of the Rosicrucian ca-
balists, the diablerie of the magic schools
of Seville, Toledo, and Salamanca ; the
domestic visions which would offer us their
services when we visit Lucian's city of
dreams, and that legion of insinuating
spirits of which we have so profuse a
catalogue in a book entitled " Egregious
Popish Impostures," published in 1603.

We can readily appreciate those phan-
tasms which are the offspring of former
real impression, however they may have
been subsequently warped or magnified.
The vision of Marcus Brutus, on the eve
of the battle of Philippi, was the united
work of remorse and of apprehension, and
I doubt not that the larva or evil spirit
of a Cæsar has been again and again a
midnight visitant in the tent of many a
modern Brutus. There are some cases re-

I

corded, in which the spectral illusion has evidently been the effect of disordered imagination on some natural disposition of the individual.   Some of these will appear in the similitude of atmospheric phenomena.   This was the illusion of Benevenuto Cellini.

" This resplendent light is to be seen over my shadow, till two o'clock in the afternoon, and it appears to the greatest advantage when the grass is moist with dew. It is likewise visible in the evening at sunset.   This phenomenon I took notice of when I was at Paris, because the air is exceedingly clear in that climate, so that I could distinguish it there much plainer, than in Italy, where the moists are much more frequent, &c."   A consciousness of superior talent, and probably the homage which was paid him, even by the members of the holy conclave, were the springs of this flattering vision.

That destructive brain-worm, Demono-

mania, is often excited in the mind of a pro-
selyte, by designing religious fanatics. Let
the life of the selected person be ever so
virtuous and exemplary, she, (for it is
usually on the softer sex that these impostures are practised,) becomes convinced of the influence of the demon over
her, and she is thus criminally taught the
necessity of conversion,—is won over to
the erroneous doctrine of capricious and
unqualified election.

These miseries, however, do not always
spring from self-interested impostors.—
The parent and the nurse, in addition to
the nursery tales of fairies and of genii,
too often inspire the minds of children
with these diabolical phantoms. The
effect is always detrimental, too often permanently destructive. I will quote one
case from the fourth volume of the Psychological Magazine, related by a student
of the University of Jena : " A young
girl, about nine or ten years old, had spent

her birth-day, with several companions of
her own age, in all the gaiety of youthful
amusement.   Her parents were of a rigor-
ous devout sect, and had filled the child's
head with a number of strange and horrid
notions about the devil, hell, and eternal
damnation.   In the evening, as she was
retiring to rest, the devil appeared to her
and threatened to devour her, she gave a
loud shriek, fled to the apartment where
her parents were, and fell down apparently
dead at their feet.   A physician was called
in, and she began to recover herself in a
few hours.   She then related what had
happened, adding, that she was sure she
was to be damned.   This accident was
immediately followed by a severe and te-
dious nervous complaint."

I have here, of course, confined my observations to those spectra excited *pos-
terior* to the retina, from recurrence of
ideas, or imagination, in which the illusion remains, and is often more decisive

9

when the external sense is shut. Erroneous perceptions will occur from diseases
of the external senses, as from the incipient
disorganization of the *lens* or the *capsule*
in cataract, &c.   There are other spectral
illusions also, founded on the principles
of optics—the refraction of rays, &c.,which
being merely *substantial* and not *mental*
impressions, cannot form a part of my
subject.   Such are the appearance of two
moons or of mock suns—the Schattenmann
or Spectre of the Brocken—the phos-
phorescence of the marshes, called Jack-
o'-lanthern, Will-o'-the-wisp, or friar rush,
and the " Fairy morgana" of Sicily.

The most imposing species of spectral
illusion is the faculty of the professed
ghost seer,—

SECOND SIGHT.

A SUPERSTITION almost limited to the
soi-disant prophets of Caledonia.   The
supernatural influence attached to this

faculty is said to have gained over the
powerful mind of Johnson, who confessed that " he had now come to
think it not fortuitous." Johnson, however, was a strict spiritualist, and it is
probable, as Boswell himself says, that
" he wished for more evidence of spirit in
opposition to materialism." The sage
was, also, mighty superstitious, and constantly affirmed his conviction that he
should run mad himself : this augury
failed, and therefore the prophetic nature
of second sight needs more convincing
proof than the creed of Johnson. But the
truth is, that with regard to ghost-stories,
Johnson's belief was somewhat like the
coffin of Mahomet, perfectly poised between the negative and affirmative of
apparitions. " Yes, madam," he said to
Miss Seward, " this is a question which,
after five thousand years, is still *unde-
cided :* a question, whether in theology or
philosophy, one of the most important that

can come before the human understanding."—*Boswell's Life of Johnson*, vol. iv.
p. 285.

In the consideration of this question in
the study of psychology, it has been an
error to conclude that, because in some
certain works arguments are adduced by
imaginary characters in support of the
appearance of departed spirits, such was
the positive belief of their authors. If
then, for instance, the arguments of Imlac
in Rasselas, which aim at the proof of
spectral reality, be adduced as an evidence
of Johnson's own belief, I might observe
that it were equally rational to identify
the minds or dispositions of Massinger
and Sir Giles Overreach, of Shakspeare
and Iago

The phenomena of second sight are
rather interesting than wonderful. It is
true, there are some curious coincidences,
as in the ancient legend of the Tyrone
Family, but they may be explained on

natural causes, even to the mark on the arm.   It is a precept in philosophy never to seek for more causes than the explana- tion of the fact requires. The prophetic spectre of Lord William Petty, at Bowood, on the eve of his dissolution, although credited by some literary characters, is but a specimen of that rare coincidence, which is the combined effect of feeling and of fancy, in sensitive or imaginative minds.

Were a miracle once authenticated, our scepticism might cease, but we cannot be convinced of supernatural agency, unless something be done or known which could not be so by common means.   We might place equal dependence on the divination of the *Sortes Virgilianæ*, or the divining rods : notwithstanding, when a multitude of visions are seen, as in the instance of dreams, some may occasionally appear the coming to pass of a prophecy.

Although the vulgar are not excluded from the influence of second sight, the peculiarity of this presumed privilege is, that among the seers themselves it is to a degree voluntary—obedient to almost regular periods. By fixing the attention on the subject during the " dark hour," the power of divination may be increased, but not controlled. There is a spell, however, which exerts a powerful influence over this thraldom, even in its most intense degree.— Music, which

" Hath charms to soothe the savage breast,"

is fraught with fascination which casts a brilliant gleam of light over the gloom of the ghost seer. The fiend of melancholy of Saul was chased away by the harp of David, and the dark hour of Allan Macauley was brightened by the melody of Annot Lyle.

Indeed those who indulge in the illusions of second sight, (all imaginative disorders being, to a certain degree, increased by indulgence) are often driven on by enthusiasm, to a degree of frenzy, in which they seem to endure the agonizing penalty of Frankenstein, a sensation of terror at the monster they themselves have fashioned.

" How they, whose sight such dreary dreams engross
With their own visions, oft astonish'd droop ;
When o'er the watery strath or quaggy moss,
They see the gliding ghosts unbodied troop,—
They know what spirit brews the stormful day,
And heartless oft, like moody madness stare
To see the phantom train their secret work prepare."
COLLINS—*Superstitions of Scotland.*

Second sight is but an intense degree or effort of imagination, the objects of that faculty impressing the brain more forcibly than the images of external things. Some persons, be it known, by shutting their eyes before an attack of delirium, see spectres, which vanish on the readmission of light.

The beautiful mythology of Shakspeare, of Milton, and of Dante, are but illustrations of this illusion. So consistent,

though so wonderful is the exquisite creation of the Tempest, and the Midsummer
Night's Dream, that we can scarcely
doubt that the poet saw them, and from
that vision conceived this sublime passage—

" The poet's eye, in a fine frenzy rolling,
Doth glance from earth to heav'n, from heav'n to earth ;
And as imagination bodies forth
The form of things unknown ; the poet's pen
Turn's them to shape, and gives to airy nothing
A local habitation and a name !"

Among the wonders of mythology, the
eccentric Fuseli also has not revelled in
vain. So faithfully has he illustrated the
imagination of the Gothic poets, so truly
turned their embodyings to shape, so
brilliantly has he fixed on canvas, what
Shakspeare has traced with his enchanted
pen, that there is more than presumption
that Fuseli was a ghost-seer. Blake the
artist was perhaps the most wild of these
visionaries in later times. He has affirmed,

among other strange tales, that Edward
the First has been sitting to him for his
picture, and while they were conversing,
William Wallace has unexpectedly presented himself on the field, and by this
intrusive " glamour light," marred all the
studies of the painter.

But the most curious instance of these
supernatural communions, is that of the
elegant Tasso, related in Hoole's life of
the poet. " In this place (Bisaccio) Manso
had an opportunity of examining the sin-
gular effects of Tasso's melancholy, and
often disputed with him concerning a familiar spirit, which he pretended con-
versed with him . Manso endeavoured in
vain to persuade his friend that the whole
was the illusion of a disturbed imagination,
but the latter was strenuous in maintain-
ing the reality of what he had asserted,
and to convince Manso, desired him to be
present at one of the mysterious conver-
sations.   Manso had the complaisance to

meet him next day, and while they were
engaged in discourse, on a sudden he
observed that Tasso kept his eyes fixed
on a window, and remained in a manner
immoveable : he called him by his name,
but received no answer; at last Tasso
cried out—' there is the friendly spirit
that is come to converse with me ; look !
and you will be convinced of the truth of
all that I have said.'

" Manso heard him with surprise; he
looked, but saw nothing except the sun-
beams darting through the window; he
cast his eyes all over the room, but could
perceive nothing; and was just going to
ask where the pretended spirit was, when
he heard Tasso speak with great earnest-
ness, sometimes putting questions to the
spirit, sometimes giving answers, deliver-
ing the whole in such a pleasing manner,
and in such elevated expressions, that he
listened with admiration, and had not the
least inclination to interrupt him. At last,

the uncommon conversation ended with
the departure of the spirit, as appeared by
Tasso's words, who, turning to Manso,
asked him if his doubts were removed.
Manso was more amazed than ever; he
scarce knew what to think of his friend's
situation, and waved any further conversation on the subject."

The ingenious traditions and legends of
the northern nations [1] confer a prophetic
property on these diseases of the imagination, the vision of second sight, &c.
As the Taisch murmurs the prophecy of
death in the voice of one about to die, so
does the Wraith, Swarth, or Death-fetch,
appear in the likeness of the person so

[1] Women were looked upon by Gothic nations as
having a peculiar insight into futurity, and some there
were that made profession of magic arts and divination.
Such a woman bore the name of *Volva-seidkona*, or
Spakona. They were also called *Fiolkyngi*, or *Fiolku-
nung*, i. e. *Multi Scia;* and *Visindakona*, i. e. *Oraculorum
Mulier; Nornir*, i. e. *Parcæ.—Note to the Descent of
Odin, by Gray.*

early doomed to some living friend of the party; or as in some rare instances, even to the individuals themselves. This prophecy has been deemed as certain a doom as the shaft of Azrael. Of this nature are the cases of Sir Richard Napier, and Lady Diana Rich, &c., which are related in Aubrey's Miscellanies; and the following story told by Boswell.

" General Oglethorpe told us that Prendergast, an officer in the Duke of Marlborough's army, had mentioned to many of his friends, that he should die on a particular day; that upon that day, a battle took place with the French; that after it was over, and Prendergast was still alive, his brother officers, while they were yet in the field, jestingly asked him where was his prophecy now. Prendergast gravely answered—' I shall die, notwithstanding what you see.' Soon afterwards, there came a shot from a French battery,—to which the orders for a cessation of arms had not yet reached, and he was killed upon the spot !"—Can this shallow story be cited as a prophecy ? Not until every officer on a battle-field bears the almost invulnerable frame of Achilles — *ex uno disce omnes.*"—*Boswell's Life of Johnson,* vol. ii. p. 166.

There are, however, visions prophetic of dissolution, which we can believe without the aid of mysterious agency. When the northern Indian is stretched on the torture, the combination of agony, of belief, and of hope, present him with the most vivid pictures of the blessed regions of the Kitchi Manitou. And the faithful mussulman, bigoted to his creed, may in the agonies of death, feel convinced that his enchanted sight is blessed by the beautiful Houris in Mahomet's paradise.

In that awful moment, when the spirit is

"Soon from his cell of clay,
    To burst a seraph in the blaze of day,"

the mind is prone to yield to those feelings, which it might, perhaps, in the tur-
moil of the living world, and at another
period, deem superstition. There is something in the approach of death, of so holy
and solemn a nature—something so unlike
life in the feeling of the dying, that in this
transition, although we cannot compass
the mystery, some vision of another world
may steal over the retiring spirit, imparting to it a proof of its immortality. It is
on the verge of eternity, and the laws and
principles of vitality may be already re-
pealed by the Being who conferred them ;
the arguments, then, regarding the phenomena of life may fail, when life has all but
ceased. In some cases of little children,
this unearthly, or at least unusual feeling,
has caused them to anticipate their dissolution. In other cases some oppressive
or morbid cause of insanity may be removed by the moribund condition. I
would adduce, in illustration, the case of

K

the insane woman of Zurich, mentioned by Zimmerman, who, " a few hours before her death, became perfectly sensible and wonderfully eloquent." The case recorded by Dr. Perceval, of a female idiot who died about the age of thirty-five, of consumption, who evinced great powers of intellect previous to dissolution. That also, related by Dr. Marshall, of the maniac who became completely rational some hours previous to his death. This case, indeed, seems inexplicable by mere physical causes, as more than a pint of effused serum was discovered beneath the membranes and in the ventricles of the brain.

The faculty of second sight has been often no further an imposture than in the presumption of its prophecy, and in the inpudence of the attempt to convince us of such absurdities; as, for instance, the phantom of old Booty, who was seen by his friends on Stromboli at the moment that he died in England. This Mother

Bunch's fairy tale was actually made the subject of solemn deposition.

In one of the cases related by Mackinnon to Dr. Johnson, he stated that the ghost-seer usually *fainted* as his vision appeared, a strong proof of the morbid nature of its cause.

In many cases of disordered sensibility of the retina produced by intense study, spectral illusions often occur without the slightest tendency to superstition in the patient. This increased sensibility probably causes the retina to be morbidly influenced by very minute villi or vessels in the tunics of the eye. In the case of exhausted energy of the retina, floating specks termed *muscæ volitantes* may become so numerous, as to impart a notion of films floating in the *aqueous humour*, or before the *cronea*. It is a curious question, in what portion of the retina the spectra of *muscæ volitantes* are excited. They appear

in or near the axis of vision, but as they
do not interrupt the visual rays from material objects, it is possible they may arise
on that spot, considered to be destitute of
vision with regard to *external* impression.
Or may they be produced by *detached*
parts only of the object, which impinge on
the retina, reaching the brain ?   If the integrity of certain fibres of the retina, which
by converging form the optic nerve, be destroyed, distorted or imperfect objects will
be presented.   This speck may be a
musca volitans.   Another illusion is this.
If the sun be looked at for an instant, two
or three balls of fire will sometimes seem
to roll before the eyes, and soon become
green.

In the interesting case of *suffusio scintillans*, related by Mr. Ware, in the Med.
Chir. Trans. we have a series of illusive
spectra, which will scarcely yield to the
visions in the incantations of Der Frey-

schutz, in the forms of a lucid point—a yellow flame—a fiery veil—and a ring of light.

Convinced that the presumed prophecies of second sight are mere coincidences, or natural effects, the explanation of its cause is required. When the nerve of sensation is morbidly affected, of course its *function* will usually be disordered—thus, in some cases of paralysis, cold bodies will appear heated. So by analogy, is the *function* of a nerve of *sense* disordered if its fibrillæ be diseased.

From the facility with which some of these imperfections of vision, (those which do not depend on *structural* disease in the *hyaloid membrane* or the *tumours of the eye*,) are removed by remedial means, often almost by mere amusement, we may believe that the vision of second-sight is depending on a similar *morbid* cause: the exaggerated forms and importance of the spectra arising from romantic or superstitious ideas floating in the memory. *Muscæ volitantes* are not always *substantial, i. e.* depending on points or fibres in the axis of vision, on congestions of the vessels of the retina, or of atoms floating in the humours. These specks, which do not appear alike in the eyes of all, and the brilliant beams in the *suffusio scintillans,* so varied and so whimsical, might be readily moulded into *human* form by the imagination of an enthusiast; or the feelings of the ghost-seer, who is usually morose and melancholy. These are symptoms of dyspepsia, which forms one of the predisposing causes of the illusion.

TRANCE,

&c.

———

" In this borrow'd likeness of shrunk death,
  Thou shalt remain full two and forty hours,
  And then awake as from a pleasant sleep."
                                    Romeo and Juliet.

In the derangements which we have hitherto considered, volition may be deemed a subject of secondary importance. In those most interesting cases of comatose disorder,—trance, catalepsy, and lethargy, —there is a total suspension of this function, the sympathy existing between the brain and motive nerves being lost.

In some cases of trance the principle of consciousness is also latent, the rosy

colour of the lips, and the breathing on
any polished surface, being the only signs
of vitality. In other instances, however,
the lips and cheeks are pale, bloodless,
and the body becomes cold as marble.
Hunger and thirst cease, and the whole
functions of the body are more or less
diminished. The form seems, indeed, but
the perfect work of a sculptor.

Catalepsy is an intense degree of *hysteria*, occurring usually in young females,
and depending chiefly on those states
which derange the functions of the nervous system, especially those protracted
disorders which are followed by direct
debility, or where sudden impressions of
terror have been produced. " A lady in
perfect health, twenty-three years of age,
was asked by the parents of a friend to be
present at a severe surgical operation.
On consideration, it was thought wrong
to expose her to such a scene, and the
operation was postponed for a few hours;

she went to bed, however, with the imagination highly excited, and awoke in
alarm, hearing, or thinking she heard, the
shrieks of her friend under the agony of
an operation. Convulsions and hysterics
supervened, and on their subsiding she
went into a profound sleep, which continued sixty-three hours. The most emi-
nent of the faculty were then consulted,
and she was cupped, which awoke her,
but the convulsions returned, and she
again went to sleep, and slept, with few
intermissions, for a fortnight. The irregular periods continued for ten or twelve
years, the length of the sleeping fits from
thirty to forty hours. Then arrived irritability and total want of sleep for three
months. Her usual time for sleeping was
forty-eight hours."—*Quarterly Review.*

Trance or catalepsy are diseases of
volition, as well as *incubus*[1], and some

---

[1] *Night-Mare* is but a very transient species of catalepsy—a loss of sympathy between the will and the

species of *paralysis*; some peculiar interruption existing in a portion of those
laminæ of nerves appropriated to action,
sometimes of those of sensation.

power.   In this sense, perhaps, life itself may be termed
one long and painful *incubus;* one great source of our
unhappiness being this identical want of balance.   The
actions we perform seldom reach the perfection which
the will desires.   Hence arises that constant dissatis-
faction, which even the close approach to perfection of
some of the most accomplished professors of art and
science cannot avert.

We must confess with Socrates, that the extent of
our knowledge is indeed but a conviction of our igno-
rance.   The metaphor of Sir Isaac Newton, on the
insignificance of his own scientific attainments, is well
known.   Sir Joshua Reynolds so highly appreciated
perfection in his art, that he was ever discontented
with his own paintings, and frequently, by repeated
touches, destroyed the effect of a picture which had
been, in its early stages, beautiful.   And Dr. Johnson,
after astonishing the world with his perfect specimen
of lexicographical composition, confessed that he " had
not satisfied his own expectations."

May I add to these, the discontent of the unrivalled
Paganini ?

With all this disturbance it is strange that
consciousness may be so little impaired—
it is sometimes as perfect as in a state of
health. The descriptions which patients
themselves give of these sensations might
seem, as it were, the visions of departed
spirits, so unearthly do they appear to the
mind. Of these descriptions, the following is well authenticated: they are the
words of a lady who fell into a state of catalepsy, after a violent nervous disorder.

" It seemed to her as if, in a dream,
that she was really dead; yet she was
perfectly conscious of all that happened
around her in this dreadful state. She
distinctly heard her friends speaking and
lamenting her death, at the side of her
coffin. She felt them pull on her dead
clothes, and lay her in it. This feeling
produced a mental anxiety which was in-
describable. She tried to cry, but her soul
was without power, and could not act on
her body. She had the contradictory

feeling, as if she were in her own body, and yet not in it, at one and the same time. It was equally impossible for her to stretch out her arm, or to open her eyes, as to cry, although she continually endeavoured to do so. The internal anguish of her mind was, however, at its utmost height, when the funeral hymns began to be sung, and when the lid of the coffin was about to be nailed on. The thought that she was to be buried alive was the first one which gave activity to her soul, and caused it to operate on her corporeal frame."—*Psychological Mag.* vol. v.

It is to be feared that instances of premature sepulture have sometimes occurred from want of scientific discernment in these cases. This horrid catastrophe had nearly terminated the case above referred to ; and one most romantic story is related of a lady who was actually the subject of an anatomist, who, on the evidence of some faint signs of vitality, not only restored the lady to life, but united himself to her in marriage.

The case of St. Theresa, if we can believe the testimony of so accomplished an hypocrite, presents phenomena more remarkable; an *absence* of external *consciousness* with *imagination*. " Her frame was naturally delicate, her imagination lively, and her mind, incapable of being fixed by trivial objects, turned with avidity to those which religion offered, the moment they were presented to her view. But unfortunately meeting with the writings of St. Jerome, she became enamoured of the monastic life, and quitting the line for which nature designed her, she renounced the most endearing ties, and bound herself by the irrevocable vow. Deep melancholy then seized on her, and increased to such a degree, that for many days she lay both motionless and senseless, like one who is in a trance. Her tender frame, thus shaken, prepared her for ecstacies and

visions, such as it might appear invidious
to repeat, were they not related by herself
and by her greatest admirers. She tells
us, that in the fervour of her devotion, she
not only became insensible to every thing
around her, but that her body was often
lifted up from the earth, although she endeavoured to resist the motion ; and Bishop
Yessen relates in particular, that when she
was going to receive the Eucharist at
Avila, she was raised in a rapture higher
than the grate, through which, as is usual
in nunneries, it was presented to her. She
often heard the voice of God, when she
was recovered from a trance, but sometimes
the devil, by imitation, endeavoured to
deceive her, yet she was always able to
detect the fraud," &c. &c.— *Vide Butler's*
Lives of the Saints.

In the year 1738, Elizabeth Orvin slept
for four days, and for the period of ten
years afterwards, passed seventeen hours
of the twenty-four in sleep. No stimuli

were powerful enough to rouse her. Acupuncturation, flagellation, and even the stinging of bees, were ineffectual. Like many other somnolents she was morose and irritable, especially previous to the sleeping fit.

"Elizabeth Perkins, of Morley St. Peter, in Norfolk, for a considerable time was very irregular in her times of waking, which was once in seven days, after which they became irregular and precarious, and though of shorter duration, they were equally profound, and every attempt at keeping her awake, or waking her, was vain. Various experiments were tried, and an itinerant empiric, elated with the hope of rousing her from what he called counterfeit sleep, blew into her nostrils the powder of white hellebore, but the poor creature remained insensible to the inhumanity of the deed, which instead of producing the boasted effect, excoriated the skin of her nose, lips, and face."—*Quarterly Review*.

The recent case of Sarah Carter, of Shelford, near Cambridge, exhibits phenomena equally remarkable.

The return of volition is usually marked by perspiration. This is the first premonitory sign, and is often speedily followed by a piercing shriek. This is also commonly the case in night-mare, arising from a similar feeling of oppression, which causes the effort of an infant to cry as soon as it is born. From the present extent of our knowledge, cases of trance are usually abandoned to nature ; we are not possessed of the " phial of Renatus," the contents of which would speedily restore the entranced body to a state of natural faculty.

Cases of trance will, however, occur where *consciousness* is totally interrupted ; and in cases of violent *hysteria*, attended

by convulsive motions of the limbs, patients will sometimes lapse into a cataleptic
state. The limbs seem to possess a curious
property of remaining fixed in positions,
which, in a state of consciousness, would
be acutely painful. The form becomes
statue-like, and although the muscles and
joints are pliable and may be moulded to
any form, they will remain in that forced
position as rigidly fixed as the limbs of a
lay figure, or the anchylosed joints of the
self-torturing Fakir.

Van Swiëten, in his Commentaries on
Boerhaave's Aphorisms, relates the case of
a nobleman of Lausanne, who fell into a
deep sleep for six months. A sudden
restoration of his faculties then took place,
and his first question to his servant was,
whether he had fulfilled his directions,
which, in fact, his master had given him
at the moment of his attack. These cases
of protracted unconsciousness excite reflections of a most interesting nature. A meta-

L

physical question arises, of which I have
not the presumption to offer a solution :
—In what condition does the mind exist
during so long a period, uninfluencing,
and uninfluenced by, the power of perception. In cases of absolute *deliquium*, and
of *asphyxia* from drowning, &c. there is
this want of consciousness, but this is the
result of an interruption to *vital* function,
which is comparatively perfect in trance.
The restoration of this function will be
naturally followed by the phenomena of
mind, even in

" Th' Egyptian who had nine hours lain dead."

Still, there is this similarity in the two
cases, that stimuli, *mental* in the one, and
material in the other, will restore suspended vitality.

Catalepsy, especially that produced by
terror, sometimes terminates in death.

It is a problem not to be solved, the
enquiry at what moment would the mind

cease to influence the body, if there be no
recovery from the trance? It is not at the
moment when the body *seems* dead, for
consciousness may be for a time suspended
by mere cold, but at that point, unknown
to us, at which the spark goes out—when
the vital principle is not excitable—when
not even the irritability, the *vis insita* of
Haller remains. Beyond this — of the
transit of an immaterial spirit, as of the
doctrine of final causes, and the endeavour to reconcile the *apparent* paradox,
*the omniscience of the Deity with the free-
agency of the creature,* although convinced
of the sublime truth, we know nothing.

In the milder cases of lethargy, which
we see in plethoric and indolent persons, these may usually be roused from
their stupor, but the faculties continue
imperfect, and they relapse speedily into
their former state.

The most interesting circumstance in
the trance, is the power of remaining for

so long a time without the supply of
food.

We know, however, that in *natural* sleep,
the functions of the body are impeded, or,
to a degree, impaired. Among the rest,
digestion is suspended, or at least imperfect, although the experiment of Professor
Harwood with the dogs may appear, at
first, to prove the contrary.

Sleep, then, may be considered a state
of *debility*, like the slender vitality of in-
fants, who, even in a state of health, seem
frequently scarcely to breathe. The circulation is materially influenced in sleep,
the pulse being slower and more feeble
than during waking; the relaxation of the
cutaneous vessels inducing frequent perspiration, especially in debilitated systems,
and in the last stages of adynamic fevers.
With this imperfection of function, there
is a corresponding inaction; thus, as there
is little waste of the system, there is no
necessity for repletion: vitality can be

supported by a very inconsiderable action of the heart, a very minute current of blood.

Somewhat analogous to this state is the torpidity of the marmot and the dormouse, and other hibernating animals. Their activity has been chilled, and, therefore, the necessity for food has ceased; the absorption of fat, proved by their becoming attenuated, being sufficient for the supply of this slight want.

In the trance, then, there is no active corporeal power, and the function of the brain is suspended. That this function tends much to exhaust the body, is proved by the obesity of thoughtless people, of children, and of some idiots ; in contrast with the wan visage of the philosopher, who, like

" Yon Cassius, has a lean and hungry look."

In addition to these proofs, I may allege, the little food that idiots require, the in-

frequency of their sleep being also ac-
counted for, the inertness and apathy of
the brain preventing fatigue.   In very old
persons these relative deficiencies are daily
presented to our notice.

The body of the cataleptic patient, in
short, approaches the condition of less
complex animal life, in which there appears a much greater simplicity of organization; and we well know, as we descend
in the scale of creation, towards the cold-
blooded, single-hearted animals, and especially if we reach the zoophyte, in how
exact a proportion to this simplicity of
structure, is the tenacity of life increased.
As somnambulism may result from a *re-*
dundancy of nervous energy, trance and
catalepsy, as well as *incubus,* seem to
arise from an *inefficient* secretion or supply of this quality, in whatever it may
consist, or an impediment to its transmission from the *sensorium* to the expansion of a nerve.   Thus the motive power

of a muscle is, in these diseases, *suspended*, which, in paralysis, may be *permanently* impaired or destroyed.

In all these instances of trance, catalepsy, lethargy, and incubus, as well as asphyxia, we may assign as one great cause of this deficient energy of brain and nerves, the congestion of venous blood about the brain, and in the right side of the heart. This is the condition of those who die in a state of asphyxia, in which, however, there is a total stagnation of blood, while in trance and catalepsy, circulation is reduced to an extreme of *lentor* without its total cessation.

Our reasoning on this point, however, must be here limited, until we have more decisive notions of the *nature* of nervous influence.

In the course of this essay, I have presumed neither to enter deeply into metaphysical reasoning, nor to describe minutely the condition of the brain; and I

have alluded but slightly to the supposed
function of its varied structures. Lord
Bacon has observed, " He who would
philosophize in a due and proper manner,
must *dissect* nature, but not *abstract* her,
as they are obliged to do who will not
dissect her." Dissection, in its anatomical sense, however, has not, perhaps
cannot, elucidate the coincidence of symp-
tom and of pathology, in cases which so
seldom prove fatal, and the causes of
which may be so evanescent. Still it is
only by a combination of metaphysical
argument and anatomical research, with
the essential aid of *analogy,* that the
phenomena and diseases of mind can be
fairly investigated. We must believe that
each illusive representation is marked by
some change in some certain portion of
the brain, the function of which bears a
reference to the subject or nature of the
illusion. The research is one of the
deepest interest, both in regard to morality

and disease, as it must be the fervent hope
of every philanthropist, to arrive as nearly
as possible to that Utopian existence,

" Ut sit mens sana in corpore sano."

Until, however, the pathology of the **brain**,
in connection with illusion, shall be more
practically demonstrated, our conclusions
must be most imperfect.   We may argue
fluently on the *nature* of mind contrasted
with that of matter ; but, if desired to *de-
fine* it, we can only answer, that it is a
combination of faculties, and their sympathy with the senses.   We are totally
ignorant in what especial part or texture of
the brain is seated the essence itself, as
we may imagine, of the mind—the principle of *consciousness*.   On this point, if
indeed such point be more than imaginary,
the whole phenomena of intellect must
turn.   But even if we can ever hope to
determine this locality, it will be long,
very long, ere the student of psychology

will rise from his studies with the triumphant exclamation " Τελος"—ere he conclude his deepest researches without the humiliating confession,

" There are more things in heaven and earth, than are dreamt of in our philosophy."

THE END.

GILBERT & RIVINGTON, Printers,
St. John's-square, London.

For EU product safety concerns, contact us at Calle de José Abascal, 56–1°,
28003 Madrid, Spain or eugpsr@cambridge.org.

www.ingramcontent.com/pod-product-compliance
Ingram Content Group UK Ltd.
Pitfield, Milton Keynes, MK11 3LW, UK
UKHW012340130625
459647UK00009B/426